About the

Paul B. Kidd is a Sydney-based author, photo-journalist, magazine editor, Radio 2UE broadcaster and freelance *60 Minutes* researching producer who specialises in Australian true crime, fishing, humour and adventure.

Paul's articles, interviews and photographs have appeared in most major Australian outdoors and men's publications and in numerous magazines and websites worldwide.

Paul B. Kidd is a recognised authority on Australian serial killers and criminals who have been sentenced to life imprisonment, never to be released. The author of 12 books on Australian true crime and fishing, he lives in Sydney's eastern suburbs with his boys, Charlie and Dick.

NEVER TO BE RELEASED

VOLUME 3

Other Australian True Crime Titles by Paul B. Kidd

NEVER
TO BE
RELEASED

VOLUME 3

PAUL B. KIDD

HarperCollins*Publishers*
www.harpercollins.com.au

HarperCollins*Publishers*

First published in Australia in 2004
by HarperCollins*Publishers* Australia Pty Limited
ABN 36 009 913 517
A member of the HarperCollins*Publishers* (Australia) Pty Limited Group
www.harpercollins.com.au

HarperCollins*Publishers*
25 Ryde Road, Pymble, Sydney, NSW 2073, Australia
31 View Road, Glenfield, Auckland 10, New Zealand
77–85 Fulham Palace Road, London W6 8JB, United Kingdom
2 Bloor Street East, 20th Floor, Toronto, Ontario M4W 1A8, Canada
10 East 53rd Street, New York, NY 10022, USA

National Library of Australia Cataloguing-in-Publication data:

Kidd, Paul B. (Paul Benjamin), 1945- .
  Never to be released. 3, Australia's most vicious criminals.
  ISBN 0 7322 6963 6.
  1. Violent crimes – Australia. 2. Criminals – Australia.
  3. Murder – Australia – Case studies. I. Title.
364.10994

Cover Image: Getty Images
Cover and internal design by Darian Causby
Typeset by HarperCollins in 12/14.5 Bembo
Printed and bound in Australia by Griffin Press Pty Ltd on 79gsm Bulky
Paperback White

9 8 7 6 5   06 07

For my mate Ben Saddington, whose painstaking research has been of invaluable assistance on this project.

Contents

Acknowledgements

Thanks as always to Bob Stapleton of the New South Wales Department of Corrective Services; John Dunthorne, Governor of Goulburn Correctional Centre; Brian Kelly, Commander, Corrective Services, Southwest Region, New South Wales; Mark Wilson, Acting Superintendent, High Risk Management Unit (Super Max), Goulburn Correctional Centre; and the officers and staff of Goulburn Correctional Centre. Also to Helen Reade, author of *Little Girls Lost*; to Ben Saddington for research; and to Sarah Shrubb for editing.

Acknowledgments

Introduction

It seems that the possibility of going to jail for the rest of your life is little deterrent to some people.

With this, the third in the *Never To Be Released* series, I have now recorded a total of 48 cases in Australia where the perpetrators will spend the rest of their lives behind bars in the knowledge that no matter what, that is where they will die. (This figure includes the two additional cases recorded in this introduction, those of Mark Lewis and Joseph Attallah.)

These killers' crimes are the worst of the worst. Serial killings, child murder, pack rape and murder, the murder of police officers, mass murder and selling drugs on a massive scale are among them. Fifty per cent of the cases were sexually motivated. Others were for either revenge, robbery, greed, jealousy or hatred.

But, more disturbingly, in many cases there is no logical reason at all. These cases were the grisly handiwork of homicidal psychopaths, those killers with personality disorders marked by antisocial thoughts and behaviour.

In some of the cases in this book, murder could clearly be seen as the next progression in a criminal's career but authorities could do little to stop it. Peter Norris Dupas is a good example of this. Every time Dupas was released from prison for rape he re-offended almost immediately. Psychiatrists and prison authorities suspected that it was only a matter of time before he killed someone. He did. A young woman. In the most horrific circumstances imaginable.

1

Introduction

Or Leonard John Fraser. Before he was jailed for life in 2000 for the abduction, rape and murder of a 9-year-old girl, Fraser had spent almost 20 of the preceding 22 years behind bars for violent sex offences. In 2003, he was also convicted of the 1999 serial murders of three women.

Or Leslie Alfred Camilleri, who, with 146 convictions for almost every crime in the book and while on bail for sex offences against an 11-year-old girl, in company with Lindsay Beckett abducted, raped and murdered two schoolgirls. With Camilleri, who was a violent bully, murder had always been a possibility. He cost this world — and most particularly their families and friends — two young women who had only just begun their adult lives.

In other cases murderous intent was not apparent at all. Katherine Mary Knight, who had never come to police attention for anything other than a minor charge as a juvenile and occasional domestic disputes, took to her de facto with a boning knife and skinned him in the one go, hung the 'pelt' in the doorway and cooked his head in a pot on the kitchen stove.

Or Mark Mala Valera. With no criminal history whatever, 19-year-old Valera walked into a police station and confessed to murdering two men and mutilating their corpses. Then, apparently at Valera's behest — Valera was in jail by then — his best mate murdered Valera's father.

And yet again, life behind bars can come as a result of a robbery gone horribly wrong. Ian Craig Styman and Peter David Taber robbed an elderly lady in her home, tied her up and rang 000 to come and rescue her after they had gone. When 000 didn't turn up, it took 10 days for their victim to die.

Or take Bandali Michael Debs and Jason Joseph Roberts, who were casing a restaurant to rob when they were approached by two police officers who had been staking out the restaurant. They gunned the policemen down in cold blood.

And there is more murder in tandem. There is the case of Mark Lewis, 62, who was sentenced to life imprisonment without parole from 28 April 1999. On St Valentine's Day — 14 February 1994 — Lewis, in the company of Lindsey Robert Rose, was involved in the murder of his de facto wife, Kerrie Pang, a massage parlour worker. A fellow worker, Fatima Ozonal, was also murdered, because she happened to be in the massage parlour at the time. The parlour was then set on fire. On 9 June 2000, in the NSW Supreme Court, Lewis was sentenced to life by Mr Justice Ireland. (The case of Lindsey Rose was covered in *Never To Be Released Volume 2*, under the title 'The St Valentine's Day Murderer'.)

Greed was the downfall of Joseph Attallah, 48, who was sentenced to life without parole on 11 May 2001. Attallah became the first person in New South Wales to receive two life sentences for trafficking drugs when he was sentenced in Downing Centre District Court by Judge Cecily Backhouse on 6 August 2003.

Attallah was given one life sentence for trafficking $925,800 worth of heroin, and a second life sentence for trafficking $2,160,200 in cocaine. He made a living trafficking drugs through his brothel, Eternity Escorts, at Campsie, in Sydney's western suburbs. The drugs were supplied to prostitutes and clients of Eternity Escorts and street prostitutes. Attallah had been charged by a NSW Crime Agencies taskforce, which had been set up to investigate drug trafficking and other crimes in the notorious Telopea Street, in Punchbowl.

In Australia these days, the term of life imprisonment without a fixed parole period means exactly that — life behind bars. Of all the cases in the *Never To Be Released* series, only two killers who were sentenced to life imprisonment have walked from prison free men. But both were exceptional cases.

On 1 May 1997, Archibald 'Archie' Beattie McCafferty was taken from Berrima prison to Sydney airport, where he was put on a plane and deported back to his native Scotland, much to the disgust of the Scottish authorities. It seemed Archie had never bothered to become a naturalised Australian, even though he had arrived in Australia as a child.

McCafferty was the infamous 'Kill Seven' serial killer, who, in 1973, in Sydney's western suburbs, brought about the murder of three complete strangers — in order to avenge the suffocation death of his 6-week-old son Craig, he said. The drug-addled McCafferty claimed that his infant son had instructed him, from the grave, to kill seven people, and then they (McCafferty and his son) would be reunited. Archie was locked up and they threw away the key.

McCafferty's crimes were committed long before 1989, when the truth-in-sentencing legislation was introduced in New South Wales. After 20 years in prison, Archie exercised his right to appeal for a non-parole period to be fixed. He was released after serving almost 25 years, and then conveniently, and quickly, got rid of. Truth-in-sentencing legislation, however, meant that from then on, a *life* sentence meant exactly that.

The other one who left prison is John David Lewthwaite, who in 1974 killed 5-year-old Nicole Margaret Hanns. He stabbed her 17 times, with so much force that some of the blows went right through her tiny body, inflicting injuries to her heart, lungs and liver.

Lewthwaite, who was 18 at the time of the killing, was a homosexual paedophile who back in 1972, when he was only 16, had watched through a window as Nicole's 9-year-old brother, Anthony Hanns, had a bath at his parents' home in Greystanes in Sydney's west. Lewthwaite fantasised about murdering the boy's parents and abducting, raping and murdering the lad, and about two years later returned to the Hanns' house to carry out his evil plan.

Late on the night of 26 June 1974, Lewthwaite, who was at the time on parole after serving 15 months of a 6-year sentence for arson, silently broke a window and removed all the jagged glass, selecting a long sliver to use as a knife on his intended victims. Once inside the house he replaced the glass with a long kitchen knife.

He was interrupted by Nicole waking up, so he murdered her and fled, his original plan of murder, abduction and rape thwarted. Police who found the murder weapon in the backyard said that the attack on the little girl had been so violent that the knife had been bent into the shape of a horseshoe.

Lewthwaite gave himself up the following day, and at his trial was sentenced to life imprisonment. In handing down the sentence, Justice Slattery added: 'Regrettably, there is no future for you in society, and unless medical science can come up with a solution, there appears to be no solution to your psychiatric problems. The ferocity and extent of the particularly savage killing of the child indicate you are not capable of ever leading a normal life in the community.'

But as Lewthwaite had committed the murder before the introduction of truth-in-sentencing, he was eligible to have a non-parole period set after he had served 20 years, and in July 1992, his life sentence was reduced to a minimum of 20 years, making him eligible for parole from 25 June 1994.

Despite rigorous campaigning by Nicole Hanns' mother, Gwen, each year when Lewthwaite appeared before the parole board to apply for release, she could only hold off the inevitable for so long, and on 21 June 1999 he was released on parole.

John Lewthwaite lives in the Sydney metropolitan area and works as a process worker; he has not come to the attention of police since his release.

The Shirley Conlon case didn't warrant a chapter in the *Never To Be Released* series because, even though sentenced to life, a non-parole period had been set for her. It is worth mentioning here, however, as I feel it is relevant in the history of 'never to be released' cases. These are the circumstances. Shirley Ann Conlon, as a 22-year-old, murdered her rent collector in 1978 in barbaric circumstances, and as a result was sent to jail for life by Justice Slattery, who added that Conlon 'should hold no expectation of ever being released'. Justice Slattery also sentenced Conlon to an additional 20 years for armed robbery with wounding.

In April 1992, the same Justice Slattery reduced Conlon's life sentence to a minimum of 15 years' jail. She was released in 1993. Justice Slattery played an important part in Conlon's release, as he conducted an extensive examination into the woman's deprived upbringing before presiding over her application to have her life sentence reduced to a determined minimum.

As I have pointed out, Archie McCafferty, John Lewthwaite and Shirley Ann Conlon are the exceptions to the rule. But they were never sentenced to life imprisonment with the judges' recommendation that they were 'never to be released'. The law in New South Wales has now been changed — anyone sentenced to life imprisonment without parole prior to the 1989 truth-in-sentencing legislation will now die there. The prisoners in this group are:

- Allan Baker and Kevin Garry Crump, for the 1973 abduction, rape and conspiracy to murder of Virginia Morse while she was alone on her family property at Collarenebri in western New South Wales (Virginia Morse's murder actually took place over the border in Queensland);
- John Raymond Travers, Michael James Murdoch, Lesley Joseph Murphy, Michael Patrick Murphy and Gary Stephen Murphy, for the 1986 abduction, rape and murder of Anita Cobby in western Sydney; and
- Stephen Wayne Jamieson, Bronson Matthew Blessington and Matthew James Elliott, for the 1988 abduction, rape and murder of Janine Balding in southern Sydney.

Of the other criminals I have written about in this series, two have committed suicide in jail, both by hanging. They are:

- serial rapist Darren Osborne, who in 1986 raped women from Queensland to Western Australia and finally murdered a woman in Albany; and
- Michael George Laurance, 46, a homosexual paedophile who murdered three schoolboys in Griffith, in rural New South Wales, between September 1984 and June 1986.

Another, Leonard Lawson, 76, who was the longest serving (on a single stretch) prisoner in Australia, having been behind bars since 1961 for the murders of two schoolgirls, died of a heart attack in his cell in Grafton jail in November 2003.

Lawson's death leaves William 'the Mutilator' MacDonald, 79, the longest serving (again, on a single stretch) prisoner in Australia. MacDonald has been in jail since 1963 for the mutilation murders of four homeless men.

In August 2000, I co-produced a segment for *60 Minutes* about the two longest serving prisoners in Australia: Lawson and MacDonald. I had come to like 'Old Bill' MacDonald through the many times I had interviewed him for my book about his life, *The Knick Knack Man*. Bill was obviously insane at the time of the killings but, almost 40 years on, he was a gentle, kind and sincere man.

But I had never met the notorious schoolgirl killer Lennie Lawson.

In the interview Lawson was initially repentant of his crimes, but the more reporter Liz Hayes probed, the sorrier he became for himself, crying as he told how hard it had been for him all those years he had been behind bars. I felt sick.

'I didn't see a tree or hear a baby cry for many, many years,' Lawson wept, telling of his years in maximum security. 'All but one member of my family abandoned me and I was all alone.'

Little wonder. In 1954, Lawson had been sentenced to death for the rapes of two Sydney models. He escaped the noose and was freed after only 7 years. Six months later he raped, battered and stabbed to death a 16-year-old schoolgirl and shot another to death in a siege the following day.

In June 1972, in Parramatta jail, Lawson held a knife to the throat of Sharon Hamilton, a member of a concert group which had come to the jail to entertain the inmates. As Lawson was dragging her away, other inmates came to the rescue and the terrified woman escaped with a number of cuts requiring stitches. But the scars were much deeper. Sharon suffered from chronic depression over the incident and six years later committed suicide.

When I heard that Lenny Lawson had died of old age, I couldn't help but wonder if perhaps they did get it wrong all those years ago. Maybe Lawson was the perfect argument for capital punishment. Had he been hanged in 1954, the world undoubtedly would have been a better place with those three young lives still in it and him gone.

And there are others who just don't learn. Even in jail. Another lifer, Vester Fernando, had his sentence increased. In 1994 at Walgett with his cousin Brendan Fernando, Vester abducted 21-year-old nurse Sandra Hoare from the Walgett hospital, took her to a nearby field and raped and murdered her. Both were sentenced to life without parole. On 22 September 1999, Brendan

Introduction

Fernando was fatally stabbed in Lithgow Correctional Centre. In April 2001, his cousin, Vester Fernando, was given an additional 30 years for Brendan's killing.

And it will go on. As certain as the sun will rise, there are more crimes in the future, so evil that their perpetrators will warrant the most severe penalty of them all: never to be released.

Paul B. Kidd
Sydney, February 2004

Chapter 1

MR DEATH

Paul Steven Haigh

By murdering seven people, it would appear that Paul Haigh fits into the category of 'serial killer', as defined by American criminologist Eric W. Hickey in *Serial Murderers and Their Victims* (Wadsworth Publishing, Belmont, CA, 1997): 'The definition of a serial murderer should include all offenders, male or female, who kill three or more victims over days, weeks, months or years. This cooling-off period is the critical factor that separates the serial killer from the mass and spree killers.'

But it is my opinion that Paul Haigh was not a serial killer. Haigh's murders were all in the line of business: robberies and then self-preservation. Professional killers do not fall into the category of serial killer.

For this reason I left Haigh out of my book *Australia's Serial Killers: The Definitive History of Serial Multicide in Australia*, which covered every case of serial murder in Australia from 1822 up to the time of writing (in 2000).

It wouldn't surprise me if this exclusion has offended Haigh, as I am led to believe that he revels in his notoriety. Haigh's main aim in life appears to be being remembered as Victoria's worst mass killer. His tally of seven victims brings him level with the infamous Hoddle Street killer, Julian Knight.

But to be omitted as a serial killer must have been a jolt to his warped ego. I hope so. The category Paul Haigh falls into is that of heartless psychopath: he killed innocent victims in the process of armed hold-ups, and others whom he believed would inform on him.

Two of his victims were a mother and her 9-year-old son. Another two were ordinary citizens who were just going about their business and got caught in the middle of hold-ups.

The exact date of Paul Haigh's birth — and, for that matter, his original given name — is not known, because he was found abandoned in a suburban Melbourne garden in 1958, when he was about eight weeks old. Welfare workers established that his natural parents were chronic alcoholics who abused his psychiatrically and intellectually impaired brothers and sisters.

The baby boy was adopted out to a hard-working childless couple, contract cleaner Patrick Haigh and his wife, Alice, who lived in the upper middle-class Melbourne suburb of Canterbury. The overjoyed Haighs took the tiny waif into their home, named him Paul Steven and bestowed upon him as much love and affection as any little boy could ever wish for.

Yet despite his loving home environment, things soon started going wrong. Even while young Paul was at Canterbury Primary School he showed signs of the dark side of his character, a side that would emerge with murderous results in the years ahead.

At school he was said to be a loner who didn't mix with the other children, especially girls. At 10 he was run over by a car, after which he became even more withdrawn. Within a year of the accident he had spent weeks in hospital because of two separate illnesses: viral meningitis and glandular fever.

At 13, soon after he began at Swinburne Technical School in Hawthorne, Haigh was convicted of theft in the Children's Court. At 14 he was made a ward of the state, and at 15 he was convicted of car theft. Haigh was sent to a youth training facility in August 1973 for assault.

Patrick and Alice Haigh did their best to support their wayward adopted boy, and they left the door open for him each time he came home. But each time, he ended up being taken away by the police yet again. More convictions followed and Haigh was sent to a youth training centre, from which he escaped in 1975. By this time he was an alcoholic. He was 17.

After being convicted in July 1976 of armed robbery, he was sent to Pentridge for his first stint of 'real' jail time. Out of jail on 21 September 1978, it wasn't long before he committed his first murder. A month after his release, a masked Haigh burst into the Tattslotto agency in the Melbourne suburb of Windsor. He bailed up counter assistant Evelyn Abrahams, 58, with a double-barrelled shotgun, and demanded the contents of the till. He threw a brown paper bag at Miss Abrahams and ordered: 'Fill it up.'

Obviously stunned, Miss Abrahams turned her back on Haigh and opened an office door behind the counter. 'What should I do?' she called out to her manager, who was in the office.

At this stage Haigh moved forward, saying, 'You mongrel dog,' and shot Miss Abrahams in the back of the head at point blank range. He then fled the building, empty-handed.

The power of the blast spun Miss Abrahams through the air and into the office, where she collapsed, spread-eagled on her back in a pool of blood. She died almost instantly.

Within minutes of the shooting dozens of armed detectives cordoned off the Prahran–Windsor area. More than 100 plainclothes and uniformed police took part in the hunt for the gunman during that afternoon and night. They searched houses and laneways throughout the immediate area, but Haigh had made good his escape.

On 7 December 1978, Haigh tried to rob a Caulfield pizza shop with a shotgun by jumping onto the counter and demanding money from 45-year-old proprietor and father of two Bruno Cingolani, who virtually signed his own death warrant by offering resistance.

When Mr Cingolani tried to grab a knife from the drawer behind the counter, Haigh shot him in the stomach at point blank range. Although he was mortally wounded, Mr Cingolani still wouldn't give up the fight: he grabbed the barrel of Haigh's gun as he collapsed to the floor and died. Despite a huge search by police, Haigh escaped again, and again empty-handed.

On 27 June 1979, Haigh went to an apartment in St Kilda with the intention of killing a woman he had been told had been telling police about his activities. Unfortunately for the woman's boyfriend, Wayne Keith Smith, 27, she was not at home when Haigh knocked on the door, gun in hand.

Haigh forced his way inside. When he couldn't find the woman, he decided to kill Smith instead. Haigh forced the terrified Smith onto the bed, aimed the gun at his head and pulled the trigger. It misfired, so Haigh made hasty repairs to the firing mechanism and then shot Smith in the chest and head five times, killing him instantly.

On 22 July 1979, Haigh went to the St Kilda home of Sheryle Ann Gardner, 31, with the intention of murdering her. Ms Gardner had been witness to the murder of a woman named Eve Karlson, and although Haigh had not been involved in the killing, he was under instructions from Ms Karlson's killer, escaped convict Barry Quinn, to get rid of her.

When Haigh arrived on her doorstep and told her to get into her car with him and drive, Sheryle Gardner must have known that she was going to be killed. In a desperate gamble for her life, she called to her 9-year-old son, Danny William Mitchell, to come and join them, in the belief that while she was with the boy she would be safe. It was a tragic mistake.

They drove to the nearby suburb of Ripponlea, where Haigh shot and killed Danny with a single .22 bullet to the back of the head as the lad ate a hamburger and sipped on a milkshake in the car. He then executed the boy's mother, firing seven shots into her from the back of the car as she sat in the front cradling her dead son.

Paul Haigh's girlfriend, Lisa Maude Brearley, 19, who was an associate of Smith and Ms Gardner, became his sixth victim. He stabbed her 157 times after he had forced her, at knifepoint, to have sex with another man on 8 August 1979. Her decomposing body was found under bark and branches in the Olinda State Forest, about 50 km east of Melbourne, two weeks later.

Police were appalled at the injuries, and said that Ms Brearley had been the victim of an 'extremely vicious and frenzied attack' — she had stab wounds to the stomach, chest, back, arms and neck.

Ms Brearley's blood-stained car had been found at the Lilydale railway station car park soon after she had been reported missing on 10 August. Detectives established that hours before her death, when Ms Brearley had left a South Caulfield house to keep an appointment, she had been hysterical and fearing for her life.

Detectives also found out that she had been issued with a shooter's licence at St Kilda police station on 18 July, and that she knew Sheryle Gardner — the woman who, along with her young son, had been murdered only weeks earlier.

Task force detectives working on the cases had no trouble linking the killings of Wayne Smith, Sheryle Gardner, her son Danny, and Lisa Brearley to three men — Barry Robert Quinn, Robert Lindsay Wright and Paul Steven Haigh.

At the time of these murders, Quinn had been on the run after escaping from custody while serving a life sentence for double murder, but he had since been recaptured and was back in prison. Acting on a tip-off, detectives quickly rounded up Wright and Haigh and charged them with four counts of murder. They both pleaded not guilty to all charges.

At their trial the court was told that the spate of murders began when Barry Quinn, a career criminal, had escaped. Quinn's life of crime began when he was 12. In 1960 he was convicted of robbing a garage. Within a year he had appeared before the Children's Court several times on charges of breaking and entering, stealing and larceny.

The next year Quinn was removed from his mother's home. After leaving the care of the Community Welfare Department several times, he was placed in a youth training centre. In 1963 he was ordered to undergo psychiatric assessment; the assessment found that he was not mentally disturbed.

On 26 March 1974, Quinn shot two men dead while robbing the Car-O-Tel Motel in St Kilda. He was caught, convicted and sentenced to death. The sentence was later commuted to life imprisonment.

In November 1978, he became the most wanted man in Australia after an audacious escape carried out with the help of a woman he later confessed to killing — although he was subsequently acquitted of that crime. Quinn escaped by leaping through a window at the Fairfield Infectious Diseases Hospital. He had been transferred there from Pentridge to be treated for what was suspected to be hepatitis. His escape — which had been carefully planned — was concealed for a few vital seconds by his former lover, Eve Karlson, who was visiting him.

During Haigh's trial, the court heard from the prosecution that Ms Karlson was Quinn's third victim, part of what would become a chain of increasingly callous killings; she was repaid for her loyalty with several bullets to the head a few weeks after the escape.

The police had put the puzzle together: they believed that Ms Karlson was murdered because of the jealousy of Sheryle Ann Gardner, who was Quinn's de facto wife. They also believed that Ms Gardner had been at Quinn's hideout in the bush with Quinn and Wright and Ms Karlson when Ms Karlson was murdered there, and that this ultimately led to her — and her son's — death.

The court was told that police also believed that the reason for the death of Wayne Smith was that Haigh and Wright both thought he had been talking too much about Ms Karlson's death.

After Quinn's escape and the murder of Eve Karlson, Quinn and Gardner had fled to Perth, but they returned to Victoria, where they were captured in a raid on a house in the suburb of Scarborough. Quinn had been on the run for 69 days; his escape resulted in the murder of five people.

In November 1980 Haigh was found guilty on all four counts of murder. Wright was found to have been in the company of Haigh when three of the murders took place: those of Wayne Smith, Sheryle Gardner and Danny Mitchell. Wright was found not guilty of the murder of Lisa Brearley, Haigh's girlfriend. Both men were sentenced to the mandatory term — life imprisonment — on each of the charges of which they were convicted.

On 5 July 1984, Barry Quinn died in hospital. On entering a day room of the Jika Jika high-security wing of Pentridge Prison, a fellow inmate, Alex Tsakmakis, doused him with a can of flammable solvent (used for hobby work) and set him alight. It took prison officers only a few seconds to reach Quinn and smother his burning clothes with blankets, but in that time 70 per cent of his body had been burned.

In 1986 Haigh confessed to the slayings of Evelyn Abrahams in the Windsor Tattslotto agency in 1978 and Bruno Cingolani in his pizza shop in the same year. He was sentenced to two more terms of life imprisonment.

In April 1993, Haigh was convicted of the murder of fellow Pentridge inmate Donald George Hatherley, who was serving five and a half years for aggravated rape. Hatherley was found hanged in his cell. Haigh claimed that Hatherley told him he wanted to die and that he (Haigh) simply helped the man kill himself, but the jury was informed that Haigh could be found guilty of murder whether or not his fellow inmate wanted to die.

During the trial on this murder charge, the court watched a video interview in which Haigh said that the death of Hatherley had been an adventure, and gave him the chance to kill in a new way. Haigh said he enjoyed the experience because it was his first chance to be involved in the death of a person who wanted to die.

In the video, Haigh said Hatherley had tried to commit suicide several times, and the pair discussed how it should be done. On the fateful day, Haigh found a piece of nylon rope in the jail's B Annexe and went with Hatherley to his cell. After sharing a cigarette and coffee, Haigh tied a noose around Hatherley's neck, and wished him 'good luck'. He pulled away the cupboard Hatherley was standing on. Minutes later, realising that the man had not died, Haigh put his arms around Hatherley and pulled down steadily on his shoulders, choking him. Haigh said he stroked Hatherley's chest and said: 'Let go your breath, mate.'

In a long unsworn statement from the dock (statements from the dock are not available for cross-examination), Haigh said he 'certainly did not' murder Hatherley. 'He willingly went to his death in a way that shamed me,' he said. 'I wasn't insensitive to his needs. I didn't act rashly. I certainly didn't murder him.' Haigh said in the statement that he was in court because he 'helped a man escape the malevolence of society'.

In this statement, which lasted over an hour, Haigh also told how he executed Sheryle Ann Gardner and her son, Danny. 'I shot him, along with his mother, so he couldn't say, "Paul did it",' he said.

Haigh then told the stunned court about how he stabbed his girlfriend, Lisa Maude Brearley, 157 times. Haigh said that he lured Ms Brearley to the Olinda State Forest and ordered another man who was with them to have sex with Ms Brearley before he killed her, thinking it would be 'useful' for the other man's semen to be found in the dead woman's body.

When the man told him he had 'finished', Haigh killed Ms Brearley, he said. Haigh said that he had held a knife at the woman's throat during the rape, and she had not resisted, but that she was not as 'cooperative' about her own murder.

Haigh said that he had not realised that he had stabbed her so many times, but he 'wasn't taking any chances'. 'My objective was to end her life, while she fought to preserve it. It was a new experience,' he said.

Back on the subject of the death of Donald Hatherley, Haigh said, 'I have murdered six persons in the past and wanted the opportunity when it was offered to me to see what it would be like to assist someone in a suicide ... to help them die without malice.'

Haigh said he had initially tried to conceal his involvement in this death, but that he later gave a prison chaplain permission to reveal his confession. Haigh said he had done this because he did not want to jeopardise his chances in an application to the Supreme Court to set a new minimum term for his past offences.

Haigh concluded by saying, 'My life is black in many ways, but I still have a bit of decency. If persons consider me mad, I am what I am.'

Unfortunately, Paul Steven Haigh is not mad. Were he deemed insane, there could possibly be an excuse for his crimes. He is never to be released from prison under any circumstances.

Chapter 2

MURDER TO LET

Ashley Mervyn Coulston

Ashley Coulston's life before prison — or at least what police know of it for certain — consisted of three major events. As a 14-year-old schoolboy in 1971, he kidnapped two teachers at gunpoint. In 1989 he sailed a spa-bath sized yacht across the Tasman Ocean to New Zealand and back. And in 1992 he mercilessly executed three strangers, each with a single shot to the head, as they lay bound and gagged on the floor of a house he seemed to have applied to share with them.

Police also have good reason to believe that linking these events was a series of rapes across three states — and a murder. These rapes all involved an identical technique: use of a balaclava, a sawn-off rifle, white plastic cable ties and a tendency to attack when the victim was with a male companion.

Born into the family of a prominent cattleman in the cattle and dairy farming hamlet of Tangambalanga, about 15 km south of the New South Wales border in northeastern Victoria, Ashley Mervyn Coulston was mainly raised by his two sisters, because of his mother's poor health.

From all accounts he was a sad and lonely little boy, constantly ridiculed at school by his classmates for being dyslexic. He was labelled the 'class dummy', and was caned for bad behaviour on a regular basis. He had no friends and eventually became a loner; he seemed to have learned that the best way to stay out of trouble with teachers was to keep his mouth shut.

When he was 13, Coulston robbed the local butter factory and later burgled other town buildings, including the sports pavilion. In April 1971, as a 14-year-old student, he went a step further.

He forced his way into the home of two 22-year-old female teachers. The teachers, both on their first placement after finishing college, were relaxing on a Sunday night when they heard a noise at the front door. When they opened the door, Coulston forced his way in and robbed them at the end of a .22 rifle. He then held them hostage for several hours, before forcing them to drive him to Sydney.

He told them that he had planned the abduction methodically, spending the previous two weeks stalking the house, and had been waiting in bushes for the boyfriend of one of the women to leave before he made his move.

When the women stopped the car to use a roadside toilet facility in Albury and tried to escape, Coulston coolly blocked their path and forced them back into the car. In the early hours of the following morning the trio stopped for a meal at a 24-hour roadhouse at Gundagai, about four hours southwest of Sydney. Coulston left his rifle in the car and, when some customers entered the diner, the women began screaming that they had been kidnapped and were in grave danger. Coulston remained seated at the bar and made no attempt to escape as he was overpowered by a truck driver and taken to the local police station.

Found guilty of abduction, armed robbery, being armed with felonious intent, and break and steal, Coulston was sentenced to three months at the Monaro boys' home in Melbourne, where he completed his third year of high school.

After his release in mid-1971, Ashley moved with his embarrassed family to a dairy they had purchased at Kyogle, near Lismore in northern New South Wales, a very long way from the district that had been home to generations of Coulstons. In 1979 his father sold the Kyogle dairy and moved to a property on the outskirts of Brisbane. Ashley, now 23 and a motorbike enthusiast, moved with them.

From all accounts he was a pleasant young man who was a bit shy and withdrawn. He often spoke of becoming famous and being on the front pages of the papers, and said that someday he would achieve that. He didn't say how.

It is highly probable that in the summer of 1979 Ashley Coulston embarked on a series of rapes up and down the east coast of Australia, first as the 'Balaclava Rapist' in Queensland, then as the 'Sutherland Rapist' in New South Wales in the mid-1980s.

The Balaclava Rapist — a young man clad in a black balaclava and armed with a sawn-off .22 rifle — terrorised couples in lovers' lanes and homes. He showed no fear whatever when a man was found to be present in the home of an intended victim. He had a distinctive modus operandi: he always struck at night, always bound and blindfolded his victims with tape, and always made good his escape on a motorbike.

The rapist first struck on 15 December 1979. He abducted a 30-year-old woman from her Gold Coast home at gunpoint, tied her up with tape, drove her away in her own car, raped her and left her locked in the boot.

Nine days later a young couple sitting in their car at Tweed Heads was attacked. Both victims were tied up and the woman was raped. The rapist struck again four days later at a farmhouse at Cudgen, where he tied up a man at gunpoint and raped his wife.

More attacks on the Gold Coast and in New South Wales followed soon after. Police were in the dark as to who the offender was, saying only that the Balaclava Rapist had group A blood; they stopped short of saying whether or not he was a group A secretor. (In simplified terms, a secretor is a person who secretes their blood-type antigens into body fluids such as saliva, digestive tract mucus and respiratory cavities. A non-secretor puts little to none of their blood-type antigens into these fluids. About 80 per cent of the population are non-secretors, with the remaining 20 per cent being secretors.)

In February 1980 the Balaclava Rapist murdered 33-year-old English migrant Geoffrey Parkinson, shooting him four times during a violent struggle after abducting Parkinson and a lady friend at Tweed Heads. After this, the Balaclava Rapist disappeared for eight months. He resurfaced in late 1980, and after two more attacks vanished without a trace.

In December 1980, Coulston left the family home to live on a yacht in Gunnamatta Bay on Port Hacking in southern Sydney. Soon after, he was alternating between living on the yacht and with a married couple who lived in the district between 1980 and 1987.

Ashley Mervyn Coulston

A teetotaller who had trouble keeping a girlfriend, Coulston worked as a car detailer at Hertz Rent-A-Car at nearby Mascot, and in his spare time he learnt to sail.

There were numerous attacks on women in the Port Hacking district between 1981 and 1984 that didn't show a distinct pattern, but in 1985 a perpetrator with the identical modus operandi to that of the Balaclava Rapist struck: he wore a balaclava, he carried a sawn-off .22 rifle, and he tied up his victims — whom he found at local lovers' lanes or in their homes while in company of a male partner — with tape.

The first attack by the 'Sutherland Rapist' took place on the night of 7 August 1985. A masked man bound, gagged and blindfolded a woman in her Kirrawee backyard and drove her to nearby bushland, where he raped her and left her. From a trace of his blood left on the fence, forensic experts were able to determine that their man was a group A secretor. This narrowed the field considerably.

The Sutherland Rapist's next attack wasn't until eight months later. On the night of 4 April 1986, he attacked a couple parked in a car near the Sutherland swimming pool. At the point of a sawn-off shotgun the man and woman were bound and gagged with tape and covered with hoods by a man wearing a dark red balaclava. They were driven a short distance to bushland in their car, then the woman was raped while the man was locked in the boot. From the rapist's sperm it was determined that he was also a group A secretor. A month later, another couple was attacked, in nearby Miranda Park, in identical style.

On 7 August 1986 Coulston was sacked from his job at Hertz Rent-A-Car after being accused of stalking a woman employee. The same night, a young woman escaped from the Sutherland Rapist after being gagged, tied and put in her car. She managed to get out of the vehicle as it drove off.

At 12.30 pm on 12 February 1987, a man wearing dark glasses and a peaked khaki hat and carrying a sawn-off double-barrelled shotgun bailed up a couple as they were walking through bushland in the Royal National Park (in the Sutherland district). They were bound, gagged and hooded before being frog-marched at gunpoint into the bush, where the man was chained to a tree and the woman was raped. Again, the rapist was a group A secretor.

In 1987, after years of researching nautical records and learning how to become a competent sailor, Coulston decided on a journey that was within his physical and financial reach — and that was so insane that if he pulled it off it would almost certainly guarantee him the recognition he had always so desperately craved. As his gift to Australia for its bicentennial celebration, he would cross the Tasman Sea to New Zealand in the smallest boat ever to do it.

In just under a year, and at a cost of $8000, Ashley Coulston designed and built a 2.5 m (9 ft) spa-bath sized aluminium sloop he called *G'day 88*. It was basically a cabin not much bigger than a floating telephone box surrounded by a hull. Cabin temperatures ranged from 20°C to 30°C, which meant that he had to sleep without a sleeping bag stretched out on a foam mattress that had a tilt of about 30 degrees when he was sailing in crosswinds. To cook, Coulston had to kneel while he heated food in a billy strapped to the stove.

Crammed all around Coulston were the essential ingredients of a long-distance sea voyage: gas stove, solar panel, observation dome, sleeping bag, spare domes, fuel tank, fishing reel, sweets, sail bag, spare mast, 100 m of anchor rope, 250 kg of lead ballast, 185 litres of fresh water, 100 kg of tinned food, a life jacket, an inflatable 2 m dinghy, two anchors, an outboard motor, 60 kg of dry food, about 100 books, a camera and film, a satellite receiver and other navigational gear, an AM/FM cassette player, a VHF radio, a first-aid kit, two sail bags, two clothes bags, tools and spare parts, two car batteries, an 'overboard' bag containing flares, an EPIRB (emergency position indicating radio beacon), fresh water and sea dye.

In preparation for the 7030 km round trip from Sydney to New Zealand and back to Brisbane, and with *G'day 88* looking more like a plastic diving bell with a plastic viewing bubble than a record-breaking yacht, Coulston proved its seaworthiness with a 175 km trial run north from Sydney to Port Stephens.

It was in Port Stephens that Coulston met 55-year-old Jan McLeod, a volunteer coastguard, whose job it was to monitor *G'day 88*'s progress as it wound up the coast from Newcastle before the next leg of its epic voyage. The pair hit it off right away, despite their 17-year age difference, and she kept in touch with him throughout his voyage across the Tasman.

Satisfied that any pre-journey bugs had been ironed out on the trip to Port Stephens, on Australia Day 1988 Coulston sailed out of Port Stephens and headed east. Six days out and about 460 km into his adventure, he found himself in the eye of a hurricane, with 8 m swells and winds gusting to 135 km/h. The tiny *G'day 88* was pounded and swamped, and he was lucky to get away with only losing his satellite navigation system. A week later the solar panel failed, and Coulston found himself without lights or radio communication for the rest of what was expected to be a 46-day journey to New Zealand.

After encountering 11 whales up to 12 m long — which caused him some hairy moments as they cruised alongside *G'day 88* for a better look at the unusual stranger in their midst — Coulston rounded the northern tip of New Zealand in 35 days, well ahead of schedule.

As he headed southeast to the Bay of Islands and the end of this leg of his miraculous voyage, he was swept up in Cyclone Bola, which went on to cause thousands of evacuations, claim four lives, cost $46 million in damage and become what New Zealanders would later describe as the worst cyclone to hit in 30 years.

As Bola headed out to sea, it scooped up *G'day 88* in its 12 m waves and 175 km/h winds, ripped the steering compass from its mounting and dismasted her. All Coulston could do was lock up the craft, making it as watertight as he could, and hang on in the darkness of his floating coffin as it was pitched about like a cork in the wake of a ferry. It was every sailor's worst nightmare.

'I couldn't sleep for three nights,' Coulston later told *Australian Geographic Magazine*. 'I never knew what was happening. There was so much noise from the howling wind and crashing water I couldn't even hear the reports on my transistor radio. Three times on 7 March the boat was completely under water. It was terrifying.'

With a determination that could have cost him his life at any second, Coulston toughed it out in the turbulent conditions for another five days. After repeated attempts to repair his mast failed, on 12 March he reluctantly triggered his emergency beacon. Six hours later, after an Air New Zealand passenger plane picked up the signal, he was rescued by a passing tanker. *G'day 88* had to be abandoned.

While the Sydney press were scathing about Coulston's attempt to cross the Tasman in little more than a floating bathtub, the Kiwis treated him as a hero, in awe of anyone who could survive the ferocity of Cyclone Bola at sea in such a tiny craft. Dubbed 'Captain Bathtub', Coulston immediately became the darling of the radio talk-show circuit, and a phone-in appeal conducted by one of the local stations raised NZ$3000 in just three hours to help him search for his beloved little boat.

In the unshakable belief that *G'day 88* hadn't sunk in the cyclone and would eventually turn up, Coulston stayed on in New Zealand to search for her, and three and a half months later his faith was vindicated: she was found, washed up on the rocks of New Zealand's west coast, with — miraculously — very little damage.

With the help of a couple of local sponsors, Coulston replaced the mast and solar panel, and in October 1988 he set sail for Brisbane. After finding the favourable westward currents, his return voyage was much more comfortable, and despite a couple of minor storms and an encounter with a 3 m shark that insisted on rubbing its belly along the hull, he arrived to a hero's welcome in the Brisbane River.

His adventure had taken him across 7030 km — 2590 km there and 4440 km back — cruising at an average speed of just over 57 km per day. *G'day 88* had

become the smallest craft ever to cross the Tasman —
in both directions. For his encouragement of Australia's
spirit of adventure, Ashley Coulston was awarded a
silver medallion at the Australian Geographic Society's
third annual awards night.

An ensuing two-page article about the Tasman
crossing in the *Australian Geographic Magazine* described
Ashley Coulston: 'With weathered face crowned by a
curly mop of sun-bleached hair, Ashley came across as a
gentle man with an almost boyish sense of patriotism.'

Coulston loved talking about his achievement. He
trailered *G'day 88* around the country, putting it on
exhibition at boat shows, and was in great demand as a
speaker. He revelled in the attention and respect.

In 1989, after all the publicity died down, Coulston
moved back to live with his family in Queensland for a
short time. He then moved to Melbourne. His lady
friend, Jan McLeod, sold her house in Port Stephens
and moved to Melbourne to be with him. She bought
a 10 m sloop, *Gulliver*, which she moored at Western
Port Marina at Hastings, on the eastern side of Port
Phillip Bay. Ms McLeod, Coulston and their two dogs,
Little Ash and Missy, moved in to live on the boat on
Christmas Day 1989.

Coulston's main source of income was a part-time
job on the French Island ferry; he also found itinerant
work skippering yachts and motor launches up and
down the east coast and across to Tasmania. All this
time, Coulston was preparing for another challenge
that would put him back on the front pages — a
circumnavigation of Tasmania in a tiny sloop.

In January 1992, while still living on the boat with
Jan McLeod, Coulston bought a .22 Stirling rifle.

Ashley Mervyn Coulston

At 11 am on 30 July 1992, Jeanet Henstridge and Jim Ruffle went to a house in Summit Road in the Melbourne suburb of Burwood and knocked on the door. The house was where Mrs Henstridge's daughter Kerryn lived. They were concerned about her, because she had not shown up for a 9 am appointment.

When there was no response, they circled the house, noticing that the lights were still on. Mr Ruffle found a ladder in the garage and propped it up against a wall and they climbed in through an open bedroom window.

Inside they found the bodies of 22-year-old Kerryn, Anne Smerdon, also 22, and Ms Smerdon's brother-in-law, 27-year-old Peter Dempsey. All were lying face down on the floor in separate rooms of the house, with their hands tied behind their backs with cable ties. They had all been gagged with socks and executed with a single gunshot wound to the head. There was a bundle of bloodstained towelling lying around the single bullet hole to the top of Anne Smerdon's head. The deceased's wallets and credit cards were strewn around the loungeroom.

Police learnt that the trio had been sharing the house, and when Kerryn had decided to return to her home town of Shepparton, they had placed an advertisement in the *Sun Herald* for someone to take her place. Interviews for a prospective flatmate had taken place the previous evening.

Police were at a loss to explain why anyone would execute the three thoroughly respectable victims. The killer had made a half-hearted attempt to make it look like a burglary gone wrong, or something even worse:

Anne Smerdon was naked from the waist down, but there had been no sexual assault.

A month later, at about 8.45 pm on 1 September 1992, insurance agents Paul Shaligan and his wife, Anne, were walking down St Kilda Road from the Arts Centre to their car, which was parked on Government Drive near the Shrine of Remembrance.

As they got into their car, Mrs Shaligan looked out of the passenger side window and saw a crouched man brandishing a gun at her face. She screamed to her husband to lock the car doors and take off but it was too late. The gunman motioned for her to lower the car window and told her to give him her money or he would shoot.

Mrs Shaligan passed $150 through the window. Then the gunman ordered them out of the car and told them to lie down near some trees a few metres from the side of the road. He told them he was going to tie them up and make his getaway. When the gunman put the rifle down on the ground to allow him to tie Mrs Shaligan's hands, her husband grabbed the gunman with one hand and reached out and threw the rifle away with the other.

At her husband's urging Mrs Shaligan took off, and after he had wrestled the gunman to the ground — and had his finger bitten almost to the bone in the process — Mr Shaligan took off after her, with the gunman chasing them and firing at them.

The Shaligans alerted two security guards, Paul Sycam and Graeme Loader, from nearby Prince Henry's Hospital, who called police on their two-way radio and then set out after the gunman themselves.

Despite Sycam's being shot in the leg during the chase, the two guards eventually overpowered the gunman. They held him until the police arrived.

It was Ashley Coulston. The 'death bag' — as it would become known during his trial — that Coulston was carrying contained a sawn-off .22 rifle with a makeshift silencer made from an oil filter, a knife, plastic cable ties, a balaclava, handcuffs, thumbcuffs and a packet of condoms.

Ballistics tests matched the bullets from the rifle found in his bag to those taken from the victims of the Burwood massacre. The serial numbers and brands of the plastic cable ties used on the Burwood victims also matched those found in the death bag.

A search of Coulston's bedroom in his parents' Queensland home revealed a single-barrelled shotgun and a .22 rifle, plus 50 Holden Commodore car keys, dozens of room keys from plush hotels all around Australia (all accumulated while Coulston worked at Hertz Rent-A-Car in Sydney). On his yacht they found piles of magazines about serial killers and murder.

Richard Shaligan was hailed as a hero. 'I was reluctant to lie down,' he told police, 'so he pointed the gun at Anne. I could feel my whole body shudder. Words cannot describe what it is like to see your wife's face down in the mud with a gun pointed inches from her head.

'When I saw him hunched over the bag, I lunged at him as hard and as fast as I could. I grabbed him from behind with my left hand around his neck and my right hand ended up on the gun. My only thought was to give Anne time to make a run for it.

'I just knew that if we did what he wanted it would be the end of us. There was no way I was going to die without a fight. When we heard on the news that he was the same gunman who killed those three people at Burwood, Anne was physically ill,' Mr Shaligan said.

Ashley Coulston was charged with the murders of Kerryn Henstridge, Anne Smerdon and Peter Dempsey at Burwood and with various offences related to the attempted armed robbery of the Shaligans. At his trial, which was held in the Victorian Supreme Court before Mr Justice Teague in February 1993, he pleaded not guilty. Coulston maintained that he could not have committed the murders because he was visiting his partner, Jan McLeod, in hospital at the time. This was disputed by the prosecution, who claimed that Coulston could have quite easily visited his partner, thus establishing an alibi, then gone out and committed the three murders and then come back to her sick bed.

Coulston's defence also steadfastly maintained that he had lent his sawn-off rifle — which he said he kept on the boat to shoot sharks — to a mystery man named Rod Davis or Davies. An extensive search by police failed to produce the mysterious gun borrower.

Prosecutor Ross Ray told the court that police believed that Coulston had answered the ad for a flatmate, and once inside the house had bound and gagged the deceased and then murdered each one with a single shot from a .22 rifle held very close to their heads. According to police, it would have taken only between five and ten minutes to tie up and murder the three young people.

Apart from Coulston being in possession of the murder weapon, the other most damning evidence came from a prisoner who alleged he spoke with Coulston in the exercise yard at Pentridge Prison.

The anonymous prisoner said that he asked Coulston if he had killed 'the three kids'. He said that Coulston replied, 'Yeah,' and said his biggest mistake was not getting rid of the gun, to which the prisoner allegedly said that Coulston's biggest mistake was killing the three people.

After four days of deliberation, the jury found Ashley Coulston guilty on three counts of murder and of numerous other offences arising from the attempted armed robbery of the Shaligans.

Mr Justice Teague sentenced Coulston to life imprisonment with a non-parole period of 30 years. Coulston's lawyers immediately appealed, because they believed that inadmissible evidence had been presented at the trial.

In April 1995, three Full Court judges unanimously ruled that the evidence of the force which Coulston had used against the couple, his production of the knife, and wounding the security guard was inadmissible at his trial for the Burwood murders: the Full Court stated that that evidence 'could not, in our judgment, amount to evidence of similar fact and could not be used against him ... It is our conclusion,' they said, 'that much of the evidence concerning the events at St Kilda Road was without evidentiary value [and was] wrongly admitted against Coulston.'

However, evidence that Coulston's gun was the murder weapon and that the ties he was carrying were similar to those used in the Burwood killings was admissible.

Coulston was granted a retrial, and after all evidence was heard before Victorian Supreme Court judge Mr Justice Norman O'Bryan, on 7 September 1995, it took just four hours for the jury to find him once again guilty of the Burwood murders and on the other charges.

In handing down the sentence, Justice O'Bryan was not as lenient as Justice Teague had been.

'In the annals of crime, the Burwood murders will be remembered as one of the most heinous multiple killings in this state,' he said. 'Your motivation is obscure, but the evidence points most obviously to robbery and sexual gratification as your motives.'

When asked if he had anything to say before sentencing, Coulston shrugged his shoulders and said 'No.'

'In my opinion, you have forfeited forever your entitlement to live outside the confines of a prison,' Justice O'Bryan said to the prisoner. 'I am of the opinion that you should never be released.'

After the sentence was handed down, it was revealed that in collaboration with an 18-month investigation conducted by the Melbourne *Herald Sun* newspaper, New South Wales and Queensland police had analysed the attacks of the Gold Coast Balaclava Rapist and the Sutherland Rapist (who they were convinced was the same man), comparing them with Coulston's attack on the Shaligans, his murder of the three Burwood victims, and his whereabouts when the Queensland and New South Wales attacks took place. Their findings were very disturbing:

- Like Coulston, the Balaclava Rapist also preferred a sawn-off .22 rifle; four times he forced his way into homes on the Gold Coast with such a weapon.

Ashley Mervyn Coulston

- Descriptions of the Balaclava Rapist matched Coulston — especially the steel blue eyes.
- Coulston carried a balaclava, and the Balaclava Rapist always wore one.
- Coulston had taken a couple, the Shaligans; the Balaclava Rapist preferred couples as victims, tied them up in exactly the way Coulston had tied up the Shaligans, and left them face down on the ground.
- Both Coulston and the Balaclava Rapist were group A secretors.
- The Balaclava Rapist had twice terrorised couples in cars before tying them up (as Coulston did with the Shaligans) and raping the woman.
- On the Gold Coast, six attacks had occurred in three months, and then there was a break of eight months; Coulston was in hospital after crashing his motorbike for that eight-month period.
- After two of the attacks, a motorcycle was seen and heard leaving the scene; Coulston owned such a bike.
- The Balaclava Rapist murdered 33-year-old English migrant Geoffrey Parkinson in February 1980 at a remote reserve that was close to a favourite camping spot of Coulston's in Tweed Heads.
- Mr Parkinson was killed by a .22 Marlin rifle, imported from the US. Of the 1200 that came into Australia, police accounted for all but one, which was bought in a Burleigh Heads gun shop by a young man answering Coulston's description. The buyer said his name was Mark Chapman and gave a fictitious address in Park Ridge, a suburb in outer Brisbane. Coulston's

family had lived in Park Ridge until a short time earlier.

• Mark Chapman was an Australian motorbike riding champion at the time of the purchase of the Marlin rifle. When Coulston, by now a yachtsman, was arrested for the Burwood murders, he said that he had lent his rifle to a Rod Davis or Davies just before the killings. Rod Davies was an Olympic yachtsman.

Given the similarities between the Balaclava/Sutherland Rapist offences and the Victorian matters, it would be hard not to think of Coulston as the prime suspect for them. But the chances of his ever being charged in connection with the rapes or the murder of Geoffrey Parkinson are very small, because Ashley Mervyn Coulston will be behind Victorian prison bars for the rest of his life.

Chapter 3

RELEASED TO KILL

Paul Stephen Osborne

It wasn't hard to track down the killer of 10-year-old Leanne Oliver and her friend, 9-year-old Patricia Leedie, after they had been found brutally raped and bashed to death in the sand dunes at Warana Beach in Maroochydore, on the Sunshine Coast in Queensland, on 9 October 1995.

The girls had left their homes in Ilaroo Crescent, Warana, at about 2.30 pm on the day before, a Sunday, to go doorknocking in the neighbourhood, asking for odd jobs so they could earn some pocket money to buy Christmas presents for their families. They were last seen in the company of a man on the beach at around 4.30 pm.

When the girls didn't return home that night a huge search was made. Their battered and semi-naked bodies were discovered 500 m from their homes by Leanne's father at dawn the following morning. It was established that the girls had been murdered between 5 pm and 6 pm the previous afternoon. Police labelled the murders the most horrific they had ever investigated.

Police promptly arrested 27-year-old factory hand Paul Stephen Osborne at his home in Wurtulla, about

2 km from where the girls lived — his wallet was found at the murder scene.

On 31 October, in the Maroochydore Magistrates Court, Osborne was charged with the murder of both girls. He was not required to enter a plea and bail was formally refused. At his trial, held in the Brisbane Supreme Court on 24 February 1997, Osborne pleaded guilty to raping and murdering the girls.

Prosecutor Jeff Hunter told the court that on the afternoon of the murders, Osborne had waved the girls down as he was walking home — after drinking 12 full-strength stubbies of beer and smoking marijuana at a barbecue held by a workmate who lived next door to the Oliver home. Osborne was known to Patricia Leedie, and her mother, Sandra O'Connor, was also a guest at the barbecue.

Mr Hunter said Osborne left the barbecue with his de facto wife about 4 pm, intending to walk home to Wurtulla, but he lagged behind and she lost him. The prosecutor said that around this time a woman walking her dogs in the area spoke with the girls and she heard Osborne call out to Patricia. At around the same time the girls and Osborne were seen together on the beach by other witnesses.

Osborne and the two girls were later seen playing on Warana Beach, and Osborne was then seen leaving them to go into the sand dunes.

When he was first questioned about the crimes, Osborne denied any knowledge of what had happened. When confronted with the fact that his wallet had been found at the murder scene, he broke down and confessed, but said he remembered little about what had happened. Osborne told police that the two girls had raced after him, calling out that he had dropped his wallet and that he picked up a tree branch and attacked them. 'I lost the plot and just kept hitting them,' Osborne told police. 'I hit them and hit them. I don't know why. They seemed pretty nice.' The attack was completely unprovoked, he said.

He did not recall raping the girls. 'When it was over, I was just covered in blood and they were dead,' he said. 'It was just blood. I don't know how long I was out of it. I don't know whether I blacked out or went crazy or what.' Osborne did not remember leaving his wallet at the scene.

When the court was told of Osborne's past crimes, it became clear that it had only been a matter of time before the time bomb ticking inside him would explode. In September 1985, 17-year-old Osborne molested a 5-year-old girl and was put on probation for three years. Two months later he was charged with choking and injuring a 19-year-old woman with intent to rape.

On 2 July 1986, he was sentenced to six years' jail for assault. He was released on parole on 25 January 1990, after serving three years and 10 months. Six months later he was charged with common assault, wilful damage and resisting arrest after behaving in a destructive way at his adoptive parents' home, and his parole was revoked. He was returned to Queensland's Woodford Correctional Centre on Brisbane's outskirts to await legal proceedings.

In January 1991 a community correctional officer contacted the prison to confirm the dates of Osborne's coming court appearances. He was dismayed to find that Osborne had been released without any supervision the previous November, despite the fact that he had not served his previous sentence, his parole record was hardly up to scratch, and he was facing new charges.

When the officer contacted the secretary of the Queensland Community Corrections Board, he was told different things at different times: first he was told that Osborne should not have been released. Then he was told that Osborne had served the equivalent of two-thirds of his original sentence and had been released on remission. Then the board secretary said again that the release was a mistake; a warrant for Osborne's re-arrest was issued on 27 June 1991.

In March 1991, Osborne committed another crime and was charged with grievous bodily harm. He was found guilty and received 100 hours of community service. A parole board psychologist reported that in his opinion Osborne was a threat to the community and should be returned to prison.

For police, the evidence leading to Osborne's arrest for the murder of Leanne Oliver and Patricia Leedie was a case of déjà vu. A decade earlier, when he had sexually attacked and strangled the 19-year-old woman in Brisbane, Osborne had left his bag, containing all his personal papers, at the scene.

In sentencing Osborne to two terms of life imprisonment with the recommendation that he should die in prison, or at least not be released until of an age where he could do no harm to society, Justice Glen Williams noted that in many cases of violence, alcohol and marijuana were involved.

Chapter 4

THE BEGA SCHOOLGIRL MURDERS

Leslie Alfred Camilleri

Few Australians who saw it will ever forget the photograph of Leslie Camilleri yawning as he was led away from the Victorian Supreme Court in 1999 to spend the rest of his life behind bars.

The tragedy is that in the eyes of many, it should never have been possible for this blasé buffoon to brutally murder two schoolgirls. Camilleri should have already been behind bars for a long, long time when the girls were killed. But he had been allowed to beat the justice system for a while, and was thus free to rape and murder.

Many believe that if ever there was an example of the law being an ass, the criminal history of Les Camilleri is it. Time and again Camilleri was allowed back out onto the streets on bail — the last time when he was facing 10 charges of child molestation and rape. This time the consequences were dire.

Leslie Alfred Camilleri was born in Liverpool, on the outer fringes of Sydney's working-class south-western suburbs, on 31 May 1969. Virtually uncontrollable from a very early age, Camilleri first came to police notice in 1981, at the age of 12, when he fronted the Minda Children's Court on charges of breaking, entering and stealing.

Over the next five years he became a familiar face in the courts, with appearances for 15 cases of car theft, eight charges of breaking and entering and 92 charges of stealing. By now a tall man, Camilleri was eventually sentenced to the comparatively light jail term of three years in 1989.

On his release from prison in 1992, Camilleri moved to Brisbane, where he met Helen Souvlis. They lived together until 1993, when Camilleri moved to the tiny country hamlet of Binalong, about 40 km from Yass, which is about 50 km northwest of Canberra, in southern New South Wales. Souvlis and her 9-year-old daughter joined him there late that year. In March 1994, their baby daughter was born and they moved to Yass.

It was in Yass that Camilleri met Lindsay Beckett — or 'Kiwi', as he preferred to be called. As both were drug users, and neither could self-administer needles, they would shoot each other up with heroin and speed (amphetamines). They became inseparable partners in drug taking and in any crime they could commit that would pay for their drug habits.

Beckett's history was appalling. Born in a tiny place named Opotiki on New Zealand's North Island in March 1974, Lindsay Hoani Beckett never knew his natural father — according to his family, that man raped his mother when she was 15.

Years later in court, Beckett's defence lawyer, Patrick Tehan, QC, told the jury that Beckett's stepfather was a 'wild and brutal man, particularly when drunk. The slightest matter would cause my client to be beaten.

Once, when his stepfather could not find the keys to a shed, he stabbed Beckett in the hand. He belted him with an electric cord, and one day after the family car was stolen, the boy was kicked mercilessly.'

Lindsay Beckett began drinking at 13, and smoking marijuana at 14. He left school soon after his 14th birthday and fled to Australia. At first he lived with an uncle at Colac, in southwestern Victoria. From then on he led the life of a drifter, roaming from town to town, picking up work where he could — and committing numerous offences along the way, including assault and malicious damage.

In 1982 Beckett moved in with his teenage girlfriend, Lauralee Tatt, in Griffith, in southwestern New South Wales. They had three children before moving to Yass in 1985. There the easily led Beckett soon became Camelleri's right-hand man, helping him with the odd labouring jobs he did around town and with his more sinister activities, such as standing over people for money.

Camilleri liked to hang out with younger guys he could impress with activities such as stealing and burning cars, setting fire to houses and breaking into businesses and stealing merchandise. Beckett was a willing sidekick. Their taste for amphetamines led to an increase in their criminal activities and by early 1997, sleepy Yass, with its population of 6500, was in the middle of a crime wave.

With lots of crime and very few suspects, it wasn't long before Camilleri and Beckett were picked up, and in April 1997 Camilleri was charged with receiving and possessing stolen goods and Beckett was given a suspended sentence for DUI (driving while under the influence of alcohol) and a $100 fine for offensive behaviour. In June Beckett spent six days in jail for failing to appear at court, after which he was committed for trial on two charges of sexual assault and granted bail.

In August Beckett was charged in the Australian Capital Territory with driving while drunk, and Camilleri was arrested and bailed for possession of a stolen Harley Davidson motorbike. Around this time a 15-year-old schoolgirl complained to police that Camilleri had assaulted her after he forced his way into her home; she refused to press charges, though, so the police were powerless to do anything about it.

On 25 August 1997, Camilleri was convicted in the Yass Court of receiving a stolen axe, shovel and electrical cord and sentenced to four months' periodic detention: this system applied only in New South Wales, and was set up so that a prisoner could serve his sentence on the weekends and still hold down his weekday job.

But weekends didn't suit Camilleri — he had to play cricket — so the magistrate allowed him to do his time on two days during the week. However, he rarely turned up. Though jail authorities were required to chase up all 'no shows', they never did with Camilleri.

Incredibly, during this time of periodic-detention dodging, Camilleri appeared in court a number of times on more charges. Because the court was not informed of his breaches of the periodic-detention orders, he continued to be given bail.

Even more amazing was the fact that during this time Camilleri was also on bail — and had been for almost two years — for very serious child-sex offences. On 8 September 1997, Camilleri eventually appeared before Judge Frederick Kirkham in the Queanbeyan District Court on 10 counts of child molestation, including six of sexual intercourse with an 11-year-old girl. Camilleri had originally been charged with these offences on 4 October 1995.

From the witness box, the child told the court that over a period of 12 months Camilleri had molested and penetrated her a number of times while she was in his care. Once, she said, he had forced her to perform oral sex on him. 'He was counting while I sucked him and every time my tooth touched it [his penis] he said that I had to do it again,' the girl told the court. It was a humiliation that a jury would hear again in the future, under even graver circumstances.

But when the trial was in its second day, 300 km away in Sydney, the New South Wales Minister for Police, Paul Whelan, gave a speech to launch Operation Paradox, a child sexual assault phone-in line. In his speech, Mr Whelan claimed that research revealed that child molesters attacked an average of 37 children before they were caught and brought to trial.

Mr Whelan said that his comments were not directed towards any specific case either in the past or pending, and that the statistics he stated were merely an attempt to emphasise the number of child abuse cases not being reported to the police.

The statement had nothing whatever to do with Camilleri's trial, but Camilleri's defence drew it to the judge's attention, arguing that despite not referring directly to Camilleri, the minister's comments may have influenced the jury. The judge then asked the jury forewoman whether or not the jury had discussed the comments or the minister.

'No,' she replied.

At that stage it was concluded that there was no justification for dismissing the jury. However, the defence continued to argue that the decision not to abort the trial carried with it the risk of a miscarriage of justice.

When asked for their opinion, the prosecution, who could either challenge the apparently trivial objection or leave it to the judge to decide, stunned the court by choosing to leave the decision to Judge Kirkham.

Judge Kirkham said that he agreed with Camilleri's defence counsel that Mr Whelan's remarks had been 'extraordinarily prejudicial to persons accused of this type of crime in general by its unequivocality. The statement also sweeps aside the presumption of innocence inherent in our criminal justice system, branding as it does all persons charged with sex offences with offences for which they had not been charged.'

He dismissed the jury, aborted the trial and released Camilleri on bail to be retried at a later date with a new jury. Within three days Camilleri and Beckett had abducted and raped a woman. Just under a month later, on 5 October, Nichole Collins, 16, and Lauren Barry, 14, went missing at about 10 pm after walking along the Snowy Mountains Highway towards their homes at Kalaru, near Bega, just north of the Victorian border in southern New South Wales.

Freed on this technicality, Camilleri's dream run continued. On 13 October he was arrested in Bega on charges of possessing stolen goods and possessing house-breaking implements. Again released on bail, this time on two conditions: that he report to the Bega police station each Monday and Friday and that he stay at a home at Bega. Camilleri obliged only a couple of times.

On 26 October Camilleri was arrested by police in Manly, on Sydney's northern beaches, and charged with possession of house-breaking implements. He was also put before the court for breaching the Bega bail conditions. Yet again he was released on bail.

On 30 October 1997, Camilleri was arrested in Hall, just outside the Australian Capital Territory, for breaching his bail conditions, and the following day Goulburn Court Magistrate Gary Jerram had him locked up in Goulburn jail. As self-confident as ever, Camilleri appealed to the Sydney Supreme Court to have the magistrate's decision overturned.

But Leslie Camilleri's dream run had come to an end. At 29, after 17 years of crime and 146 convictions for almost every crime in the book — convictions that had resulted in only a little over 3 years of prison time — he would never be a free man again. Police wanted to have a chat with him about the murders of the two missing Bega schoolgirls.

The disappearances of Nichole Collins and Lauren Barry had been a front-page story across the nation, but after a week police didn't have a clue as to their whereabouts. They had appealed for help from the public, and sightings had been reported from as far away as Western Australia. All leads were followed up, no matter how bizarre, but they all amounted to nothing.

Police even set up a road block at the last place the girls had been seen, and two mannequins were dressed like Nichole and Lauren in an attempt to jog the memories of passers-by. Nothing. After three weeks they wound down the operation, codenamed DALOA. It was soon after that they had their first sniff of a breakthrough.

A 35-year-old informant came forward and told police in Canberra about a couple of local criminals named Beckett and Camilleri. He had known them for a few months, had purchased amphetamines and sold stolen goods for them, and now shared a unit with Beckett.

The informant told police that he hadn't seen either Camilleri or Beckett on the weekend that the girls went missing, but on the afternoon of 7 October they had arrived back at the flat in Yass, and while reading an article in the paper about the missing girls, Camilleri had said, 'I bet they try and pin this on me.'

The informant had remained silent, as Camilleri had already threatened to break his legs and burn his parents' house down over another matter. He didn't want any more trouble. But now that he realised that there was a distinct possibility that Beckett and Camilleri had been involved in the girls' disappearance, he had come forward.

He went on to say that on the long weekend the girls disappeared, Beckett and Camilleri went to Canberra in Camilleri's Ford Telstar and stole a Hyundai and a Laser. On their return to Yass, Camilleri had ordered Beckett and the informant to clean out his Telstar, which was like a pigsty inside, and not to leave a trace of dirt or they would be bashed.

The informant told police that shortly before the girls went missing, Camilleri and Beckett had stolen his (the informant's) clothes and a pink television set in lieu of money he owed them for drugs.

Camilleri's de facto was also questioned by police. She confirmed parts of the informant's statement but refused to believe that her de facto was involved with the missing girls.

Police decided that it was time to have a chat with Camilleri and Beckett. Neither was hard to find. Beckett was in the Belconnen Remand Centre in Canberra for suspected car theft; he had been there since his arrest on the morning of 27 October. Camilleri was in Goulburn jail pending a court appearance over his arrest in Hall on 30 October.

On 5 November 1997, Detective Sergeant Mark Winterflood and his partner, Detective Senior Constable Stewart Gray, drove from Bega to Canberra to interview Beckett. Winterflood and Gray had been given the unenviable task of taking over the DALOA investigation. From now on it would be their job to tell the girls' loved ones either that there was no new information or that the girls' bodies had been found. It was a no-win situation.

Winterflood and Gray had decided to interview Beckett, while Detective Sergeant Joe Mura would go to Goulburn to interview Camilleri the following day. Camilleri's and Beckett's stories of events on the day Nichole and Lauren went missing agreed: they had sat in a Bega park and drunk beer that day after driving over from Yass. On the way they had stopped to collect money owed to them for speed. Unable to find the creditor, they had taken his clothes and a TV set and gone to Canberra and had a couple of shots of speed. After their return from Bega they had gone to Sydney, where they purchased heroin.

One thing that stood out was the television. An abalone diver on his way to work had reported seeing a pink television set sitting by the side of the road the morning after the girls went missing. It was near the spot where the girls were last seen. The diver said that it was not there when he returned that way a few hours later.

The detectives conferred. Could this have been the television set that was taken in lieu of the drug payment? If so, it seemed only logical that the TV would have been on the back seat of Camilleri's small car — it couldn't fit anywhere else — and it would have to have been removed in order to fit two girls in the back. Had it been left by the side of the road while Beckett and Camilleri took the girls to wherever they went and then picked up later?

With this theory and the fact that the only other piece of information they had was that someone had sighted a white car (Camilleri's Telstar was white) around about the critical time, they interviewed Beckett again. This time they were much more emphatic about the white car and the television set.

His eyes darting all over the place, Beckett was visibly agitated when the detectives mentioned the TV — the sighting of it and its disappearance a few hours later. Eventually Beckett confirmed that there had been a television set in the car; after much umming and ahhing, he said he couldn't recall what had happened to it.

When Camilleri was interviewed again the next day by Detective Mura — by now Mura had been briefed on the unaccounted for television set — his response was a dead giveaway.

'Mate, was there a television in the car?' the detective asked. The usually cocky Camilleri went silent. After a while he replied, 'Dunno. Don't know. I

can't remember. I give some stuff to St Vinnies ...'
Obviously flustered, Camilleri then described the TV
that was in his possession as 'a fuckin' square box, an
old wooden thing'. At that point the interview ended:
Camilleri refused to answer any more questions.

Convinced that they had the right men in custody
and that the TV set was vital, Mura and Winterflood
decided to go to the source — the informant Camilleri
took the television from in the first place.

But they were out of luck; the man had fled in fear
of reprisals from Camilleri. His mother said she wasn't
sure where her son was but she remembered where he
bought the TV in the first place — a local second-hand
shop. The owner confirmed that it was pink when he
sold it. The description of the TV was released to the
media. Now it was a case of waiting and hoping that
things fell into place.

In the meantime, a very distraught Camilleri was
hinting to a prison psychologist at Goulburn jail that
he was about to make a confession. He had revealed
incriminating snippets of information, and kept
repeating over and over: 'They know about the telly.'
The psychologist notified the police.

Because of his distressed state, the psychologist put
Camilleri on suicide watch; she was afraid that given
the slightest chance he would do himself in. And with a
breakthrough in sight, that was the last thing anyone
wanted.

Back at Bega, police were on the trail of the missing
TV set. A young man came forward and said he had
found the set by the side of the road and had taken it
home. When he found it to be in working order he
had put a notice about it on local notice boards; when

no one claimed it he had stripped it back, painted it black and sold it for $60 to a local motel owner. Police picked it up.

With the elusive TV now in their possession, and confirmation of the exact spot it had been found, indicating that that was where Camilleri and Beckett had unloaded it off the back seat of the car (so they could fit the girls in, it was presumed), and with the suspects in custody in separate places unable to concoct a story together, the investigators decided now was the time to strike.

They decided to play one off against the other until one broke. They would then use that against the other to find out the truth — and find the missing girls, whom they feared were dead.

Beckett's interview was conducted at the Winchester Police Station in the Australian Capital Territory on 12 November 1997 by Detective Winterflood. It began at 12.40 pm and was monitored via a remote link by other detectives and uniformed police. With pictures of the missing girls in front of him on the interview table, Beckett was told in detail what the police already knew.

Mid-afternoon on Sunday, 5 November 1997, Beckett had arrived in Bega with Camilleri — and a case of beer and a bottle of rum on the back seat of the car. Also on the back seat was a pink TV set that they had taken in lieu of drug money Beckett's flatmate owed Camilleri.

The pair had attended the Bega Festival and then, after buying some ice at the Grand Hotel just before closing time, they had headed east, towards the coastal township of Tathra. Two girls were walking along beside the road and Camilleri and Beckett pulled up and offered them a lift.

Whether they got in the car of their own accord or were dragged was yet to be established, but the police were certain that the girls did wind up in the back of Camilleri's little white Telstar after the pink TV set was left by the roadside and a pile of rubbish was moved from the back seat to the boot.

The police told Beckett that they knew all about the TV set. They now had possession of it, and it was damning evidence, albeit circumstantial, that could send Camilleri and Beckett away for the rest of their lives.

They told Beckett that Camilleri claimed that on the night of 5 October he had been given a shot of heroin by Beckett, and the next thing he remembered was waking up in Canberra later that night. He would be blaming Beckett for anything that may have happened during that time.

They also elaborated on the incriminating statements they had been given by the informant, Camilleri's girlfriend and the prison psychologist at Goulburn. They told the terrified Beckett that it was their opinion that Camilleri was going to tell the truth that afternoon in an attempt to be the first to confess — and thus first to get a crack at some leniency at the inevitable trial.

However, they said, if Beckett wanted to be first with a confession and show that he co-operated with police, and use that as a trump card somewhere down the line, now was the time to do so.

Beckett said he wanted time to have a cigarette and think about his predicament. He was escorted to the courtyard, where smoking was permitted, by the two

remand officers who had escorted him from the
Belconnen Remand Centre to the Winchester Police
Station.

As he sat there nervously puffing on his cigarette,
Beckett turned to one of the officers, Tom Collins, and
said, 'They've got us.'

'Got you for what?' Collins asked.

'For killing those two girls down the coast.'

The remark was straight out of left field, and Collins
was surprised that Beckett had decided to speak to him
rather than to the detective who had been questioning
him. But he let him continue. Beckett told Collins that
yes, he and his accomplice had dumped the TV set that
was in the car when they picked up the girls. This had
occurred in the middle of a speed and heroin drug
bender.

Collins and his partner then told Beckett that if he
told everything he knew, he could possibly do a deal
with the police and hope for some sort of immunity.

'Do you know where the girls are?' Collins asked
Beckett.

'Yes.' he replied. 'And I can show you.'

Beckett had obviously made up his mind to talk,
and couldn't get back into the interview room quickly
enough. Once in there he picked up a forestry map
that Winterflood had brought with him in the hope
that it may be of some use. 'Here,' Beckett said,
pointing to a dense forest area just over the New South
Wales border in Victoria. 'They're here.'

'Are they dead?'

'Yes.'

'How did they die?'

'Throats cut, one of them drowned.'

'Who killed them?'

'I killed them both.'

Winterflood was surprised. Not so much at the confession, but that Beckett hadn't blamed Camilleri. Usually, they blamed the other guy. Without prompting, Beckett drew a picture of the knife he had used and said that he had thrown it in Lake Burley Griffin in Canberra.

Then, on a more detailed road map, Beckett pointed out the exact route that he and Camilleri had taken. He agreed to do a taped interview and show police exactly where the bodies were. The only condition was that there would be no television cameras.

At 3 pm, a little over two hours after the interview began, Beckett, along with a team of plainclothes and uniformed police, was bundled into an unmarked white mini-bus. Followed by another unmarked police car, they set off along the Monaro Highway to the back end of the Canberra suburb of Calwell.

Along the way Beckett instructed the driver to stop. He pointed out a black patch near the road and told them that that was where he and Camilleri had burned the ropes they had used and Beckett's blood-soaked clothing.

The New South Wales detectives realised that uncertainty as to the exact location of the bodies meant that Victorian police must be immediately notified. If the girls' bodies were on the Victorian side of the border, the investigation would come under the jurisdiction of Victorian police, despite some parts of the crime being committed in New South Wales.

If charges of homicide brought by the Victorian police were not proven, there were still charges of rape and kidnapping that could be brought by the New South Wales police; Beckett and Camilleri would be extradited to New South Wales immediately and charged and tried on those charges.

Two members of the Victorian police drove up to Bombala to join the convoy, which had now grown to six vehicles full of detectives and uniformed police. They headed south along the highway through Merimbula, Eden, Pambula and Genoa until, almost 200 km south of where the girls went missing — and well into Victoria — Beckett pointed to a sign that said Fiddlers Green Creek and told the driver to stop. 'Down there,' he said.

From there they went on foot. It was just after 8 pm, and uniformed officers lit the way with torches. The track led through the bush to a tiny creek in the rainforest near the Cann River. Beckett led them through the undergrowth and fallen trees to a spot beside the creek where he said the murders had taken place.

There police found Lauren's skeletal remains, floating face down in a pool of stagnant water. Parts of her body were missing, but what was left was remarkably well preserved due to having been submerged in the cold water. She was still dressed in her jeans, leggings and striped pullover, which was up around her neck, exposing her bra.

Nearby, in a clearing, Nichole's skeleton was slumped at the base of two trees, her legs extended. She was still dressed in her Bega High School Year 12 1998 jumper. The bones in the lower part of her body had been scattered about — by wild animals, police assumed.

Lauren Margaret Barry and Nichole Emma Collins were best friends in a group of Bega High School teenagers who were all friends. Because 4 October was the start of a long weekend, and the start of the school holidays, and Lauren's 15th birthday was in a few days' time, the group, consisting of four girls and four boys, decided to celebrate with a camp on the fringe of the bush not far from White Rock Beach.

Lauren and Nichole lived not far from each other on bush blocks in the tiny township of Kalaru, population 280, which is on the Snowy Mountains Highway between Tathra and Bega. It was one of those friendly country towns where everyone knew each other, no one locked their doors, everyone left their keys in their cars, the kids played outdoors and were always home in time for dinner.

The campsite the girls had chosen for Lauren's birthday bash was at a clearing in the bush about 500 m down a rough track off the highway about 2 km from their homes. There was not the least cause for concern from the girls' parents, Garret and Cheryl Barry and Graeme and Delma Collins — the girls had camped out at the same spot at least four times in the past 18 months with various friends. Graeme Collins had set up the campsite for the kids on the Friday.

The girls would head home from time to time to wash and get fresh clothes, and their parents dropped in on the camp regularly to check that everything was okay. The kids rode their horses down to Boulder Bay and went swimming at Macarthur, but mainly stayed within the camp perimeter, talking, listening to music, reading magazines and having fun.

On Sunday night, Lauren decided that she would like to go to a party at Jellat Jellat, a small township about 7 km away. Nichole decided to go with her. The plan was that they would walk home and then get a lift to the party with one of their parents. They walked into the darkness and disappeared.

While Beckett was taking police to the murder scene, Camilleri, back to his old cocky self, was being questioned at Goulburn jail, oblivious to the fact that soon his denials wouldn't count for a thing.

'Are you going to take us to where the bodies are?' Detective Joe Mura asked.

'Yeah,' replied Camilleri.

'You'll take us?'

'Go get yourselves fucked. I'm not taking you anywhere.'

When Lauren and Nichole's bodies were found, no one told Camilleri. They left him to find out from the news on the prison TV and then wait anxiously to find out whether the girls had been found by accident or he had been given up by his mate. He would find out soon enough. But for the time being investigators let him stew.

Meanwhile, Beckett was only too happy to get it all off his chest. And in doing so he went back to almost three weeks before he murdered Lauren and Nichole, to a day when he and Camilleri abducted a woman and Camilleri's murderous intentions surfaced for the first time.

Beckett told the investigators that on Saturday night, 13 September 1997, he and Camilleri picked up a 19-year-old heroin addict in Garema Place, which at the time was the junkies' hangout in Canberra. They asked the woman if she would inject them with speed because they didn't know how to. The woman said yes, and when she was in the car they drove to the Canberra showgrounds for a bit of privacy.

When they were done shooting up, the woman asked to be dropped off, but instead Camilleri drove off in the direction of Yass. After about 15 minutes they stopped. Camilleri slid into the back — both doors had had their child-proof locks broken and couldn't be opened from the inside at all — with the woman and said, 'We're going to fuck you now. Do you want to?' When the woman replied 'No,' Camilleri pulled out a folding pig-hunting type of knife and she fell silent, apparently resolved to her fate.

All through the night they cruised around Canberra, and Camilleri and Beckett took turns raping the woman while the other one drove. In the early hours of the morning, they headed towards Sydney, stopping only to shoot up on speed and rape her again.

Once, when she started answering back and standing up for herself — when she got a bit 'lippy', as Beckett put it — Camilleri threatened to kill her by dragging her along the highway with her feet tied to the back of the car.

Beckett said that Camilleri had forced the woman to perform oral sex on him, telling her to 'Do it properly. Don't use your teeth.' Each time the woman didn't comply, Camilleri smacked her about the head. When the woman complained that she was thirsty and that her mouth was dry, Camilleri held her head back by the hair and said, 'Open your mouth,' then spat in it.

Just before dawn, as they were driving along the Hume Highway towards Liverpool, on the outskirts of

Sydney, Camilleri decided to murder the woman by throwing her from a bridge further up the highway — the bridge had a substantial drop beneath it. Camilleri discussed what he intended doing in front of her.

Fortunately for the woman, they decided to pull in at a rest stop for a toilet break, and in an instant when Camilleri and Beckett weren't looking, she took off into the bush in the semi-darkness, wearing only a T-shirt and socks.

In a statement to the police, she said that as she was fleeing she could hear them following her through the undergrowth, so she hid in a cave until she thought it was safe to come out. Eventually she plucked up enough courage to come out, and continued through the bush until she came to a farmhouse, where she explained her plight to the bewildered occupants, who called the police.

Camilleri and Beckett were still searching for the woman. They saw her go into the farmhouse, and watched as the police arrived shortly after. Deciding that it wasn't in their best interests to run — they could soon be caught and then everything that the woman told police would go against them and they would be in serious trouble — Camilleri and Beckett agreed on a plan. They ditched the knives and drugs they had in the car and drove down to the farmhouse to confront the police.

They told the officers at the farmhouse that they had definitely not raped the woman, who was a heroin addict, and that while they had had sex with her many times, it had been consensual, and in exchange for drugs. They had been heading for Cabramatta in Sydney's west to score some more drugs when she suddenly went crazy and took off. Back at the police station, the terrified woman refused to file any charges and Camilleri and Beckett were free to go.

A couple of weeks later, in early October, they were well into an amphetamine bender that had been going on for days. Camilleri and Beckett had been injecting each other up to three times a day and therefore getting little sleep. They spent their time driving around in Camilleri's battered white Telstar, looking for things to do and places to score more drugs. There were numerous knives in the car, as well as the pink TV set and a stolen chequebook.

At around 10 am on Sunday, 5 October 1997, the middle of the long weekend, they called into the Monaro Cellars in Cooma where Beckett cashed a cheque for $44 from the stolen chequebook and bought a slab of VB stubbies and a bottle of Bundaberg rum while Camilleri sat in the car out the front. The salesman observed the man behind the wheel and just in case, he took down the registration number of the Telstar — QUX 928.

Camilleri and Beckett filled in their day drinking, listening to music at the Bega Festival and driving around town, stopping from time to time to shoot up on speed. At around 10 pm they were driving up Evans Hill along Tathra Road in search of a party they had heard about on Tathra beach. It was windy, there were no streetlights and no cars coming or going in either direction. Up ahead they saw Lauren and Nichole walking in the opposite direction.

'Look, there's some chicks,' Camilleri said as he stopped the car, threw it into reverse and drew level with them. 'Where are you two girls going?' Camilleri asked. 'Do you know if there are any parties around here?'

'Yeah, we're heading to a party down the road,' one of the girls replied. They talked for 10 minutes or so through the window — Camilleri and Beckett high on speed — and eventually the girls agreed to join them in crashing the party at Tathra beach.

Beckett said that in order to fit the girls in the car Camilleri unloaded the TV set onto the side of the road. A baby seat on one side of the back seat forced one of the girls to sit in the middle. When they found no one and no party at the beach they sat around the car park, drinking stubbies and chatting.

The girls agreed to go into Bega to listen to the music at the festival, but only if they could call in at their campsite on the way and tell the others where they were going. Camilleri agreed. The girls directed Camilleri to the camp, but when the car got scratched and almost bogged on a side track, Camilleri lost his cool and started shouting at the girls.

'This is you girls' fuckin' fault,' he screamed. 'What the fuck are youse doin' bringin' me down this fuckin' way?'

Beckett told the police that it was then that he realised that Camilleri had no intention of returning to the camp or taking the girls into Bega to listen to music. Instead, he took off south towards Merimbula. As he drove he was screaming over and over at the girls, 'Shut the fuck up! Shut the fuck up!'

Still driving, Camilleri produced a black-handled knife and brandished it at Lauren and Nichole. Beckett flashed a similar weapon. Camilleri instructed him: 'If they try anything, stab 'em. If they try and jump out of the car or anything.'

Leslie Alfred Camilleri

'You're not going to hurt us, are you?' the girls asked.

'Nuh,' Beckett replied, unsure what was going to happen. He did know that he wanted to have sex with the girls, he told police.

'Do you wanna have sex with us?' Camilleri asked. The girls said no but the question was pointless — it had already been decided. Camilleri and Beckett discussed, in front of the terrified girls, who was going to have which one.

At first, Camilleri wanted Lauren, but then he changed his mind and decided on Nichole. Beckett took Lauren out of the car at knife point, lay her down on a football jumper on the ground and, although she pleaded that she was a virgin and was having her period, told her to undress and then watch as he undressed in front of her. Beckett then raped Lauren for half an hour while Camilleri was raping Nichole in the car.

Beckett told police that after this he bundled Lauren back into the car to sit with Nichole and told them to keep their heads down and stay out of sight while Camilleri drove south through Merimbula, Pambula and then along the Princes Highway to Eden.

They stopped in a secluded spot along the way and Camilleri unsuccessfully tried to have sex with Lauren after lying her on a cardboard beer carton just off the road. Then he dragged her into the back of the car, where he forced her to perform oral sex on him while Beckett drove, with his arm around Nichole in the front seat. Camilleri warned Lauren not to touch his penis with her teeth, and each time the teenager did he hit her with full force on the head with his open hand.

66

They were well over the Victorian border by now, on the Cann River Road.

Beckett told police that by then he knew that the girls were going to be murdered because Camilleri kept saying, over and over again, 'They can't go back. They can't go back. They can't go back.'

Beckett told police that Camilleri told him to turn the car off the main road at a sign that said Fiddlers Green Creek and proceed along the track, which disappeared into the rainforest. When they reached a homemade gate and the ground became too soggy to continue, he turned the car around and drove back about 100 metres, until Camilleri asked him to stop and they all got out.

'Are you going to kill us?' Lauren asked, her voice faltering.

'No,' Camilleri replied. 'We're just going to tie you up so we can get away.'

Beckett said that he knew Camilleri was lying and he believed the girls did too.

'Are you going to kill us?' Lauren asked again.

'No,' Camilleri repeated, sounding less convincing than the first time. 'We're just going to tie you up so we can get a head start.'

With that he removed some white rope from the boot and tied Lauren's hands. Inside the car Beckett tied Nichole's hands together with cloth. To be sure, Camilleri then tied some of the rope over the cloth.

'You're going to kill us, aren't you?' Lauren sobbed.

'No, we're just gunna tie you up,' Camilleri replied.

Then, with the girls being led by a loose rope hanging from their wrists, they headed into the scrub. After about a 200 m walk, they came to a creek. The water was cold but shallow, and Camilleri ordered Beckett to untie the girls so they could remove their shoes, socks, pants and knickers and 'wash themselves out'.

Beckett told police that Camilleri was screaming at the girls, 'Get yourselves in there! And wash yourselves out!'

'But it's cold,' Lauren protested.

'Just get the fuck in there,' Camilleri screamed, pointing at the creek.

Both girls hastily obeyed, kneeling in the water and washing themselves. Then they got dressed. Their hands were tied with rope again and they were led along the bank to an upturned tree that had fallen across the creek. They were told to lie face down on the bank, and were gagged.

First Lauren was hogtied — her legs were pulled up her back and the rope was wrapped very tightly twice around her neck and then around her mouth. Camilleri instructed Beckett to drag Nichole away and tie her to a tree up the bank and then come back for further instructions. On his return he was met halfway by Camilleri.

'Leave her and go and drown the other one,' Camilleri told him.

Beckett told police he replied, 'I don't wanna do it.'

'Just do it.' Camilleri was screaming.

Beckett said he protested again: 'I don't want to do it.'

'Just fuckin' do it or I'll stab ya here and now,' Camilleri bellowed. Beckett then told how he listened while Camilleri told him about the rush he (Beckett) would get as he killed the girls.

'The demon will come out of ya when you're done,'

Camilleri said, and then walked off into the bushes, leaving Beckett to commit double murder.

The police listened as Beckett explained in his dull monotone how he killed Lauren and Nichole.

'I walked up to Nichole to check and see that she was still tied to the tree,' he said. 'Then I walked back down to Lauren. All the time I could feel Les watching me, even though I couldn't see him. I stood there and called his name a couple of times real quietly, not too loud, and stayed there, listening to see if I could hear him ... I thought he might have been in hiding, just watching to see if I would do it or not. I ran down the embankment and dragged Lauren into the water.

'Lauren fought as I dragged her down to the water and held her head under. I became angry because she unbalanced me with a sort of a kick and my left knee was thrust into the water. I was angry. I took my knife from my pocket and reopened it and began to stab her. She stopped moving. Then I ran up the embankment to Nichole.

'She must have heard what I had done to Lauren, because when I got to her she said, "You're going to kill me, aren't you?"

'I told her to shut up and walked around to her left side and cut her throat two or three times. This was across her throat. The knife was in my left hand. Nichole was sitting down when I cut her throat.

'After this she was thrashing around on the ground. She was trying to scream but nothing was coming out. I think I kicked her because she wouldn't keep still. This didn't work, so I stabbed her in the throat. I aimed and stabbed at the hard thing in her neck. I pushed the knife in all the way but she wouldn't keep still. She still didn't moving so I stabbed her in front of the chest. She kept moving but she was slowing down. I waited until she stopped moving, which didn't take long.'

Beckett then described how he untied the ropes and gags from around the girls, picked up the ropes and ran back to the car, where Camilleri was sitting waiting for him.

'"Did you do it?" Les asked me.

'"Yes," I replied.

'At first I thought Les didn't believe me, even though I was covered in blood. When I was stabbing and cutting Nichole, blood was spurting all over me.

'"You did it? You didn't let 'em go, did ya?" he asked me.

'"Well go down and take a look," I said. "They're just lying down there."

'Les asked me if I had seen the demon when I killed them. It was a question he would ask me many times. I told him I hadn't. I felt like I was burning up inside. I was very tired and heavy. I was asleep in minutes.'

Beckett then described the various actions that he and Camilleri took over the next few days — burning the clothes and rope, throwing the knives into Lake Burley Griffin in Canberra (one was found by police divers the day after the interview) and cleaning out the car. Camilleri and Beckett eventually returned to Yass, then drove to Sydney.

Investigators had no trouble verifying the rape of the heroin addict Camilleri and Beckett had abducted in Canberra on 13 September. Since the pair had been arrested, the woman had been located and had given a statement about her terrible ordeal. It matched Beckett's recollection of the events word for word.

Camilleri and Beckett were both relieved of all commitments related to the minor charges for which they were being held in New South Wales and were extradited into the waiting arms of Victorian detectives, who took them to Melbourne to face two counts of murder.

On 20 August 1998 Lindsay Hoani Beckett did the right thing and pleaded guilty to the murders of Nichole Collins and Lauren Barry; this saved their families having to go through all the horrific evidence in public. He was sentenced to two terms of life imprisonment, to be served concurrently, with a minimum of 35 years; this is one of the longest prison terms ever handed down in Victoria.

In handing down the sentence, Justice Frank Vincent told the court that the life sentences would have meant life without parole had Beckett not agreed to give evidence against his co-accused, Leslie Camilleri. Justice Vincent also said that it was regrettable that Beckett was being rewarded for his cooperation with a reduction in his sentence, but it was a price that had to be paid to advance another important community interest: the prosecution of the man Beckett accused of being his partner in a double murder.

Les Camilleri was not so obliging. At his trial, which began in the Victorian Supreme Court, again before Justice Frank Vincent, on 24 February 1999, he pleaded not guilty to the murders, although the evidence against him was damning. Lindsay Beckett was the main witness for the prosecution.

Camilleri's main defence was that he was asleep when the murders took place; he had taken heroin and was doped out and didn't know what went on.

According to his lawyer, Camilleri did no evil, saw no evil and heard no evil.

When confronted with this defence, Beckett told the court, 'That's a lie. Les was in front of me the whole time we were walking down the river.'

On 11 April 1999, after a seven-week trial that called 180 witnesses, the jury returned a guilty verdict after seven hours of deliberation. There was a short burst of applause from the packed gallery when the verdict was read out.

Justice Vincent handed down the sentence on 27 April 1999 and was scathing about Camilleri. 'It seems that you were attracted by the idea of raping a 14-year-old virgin and you selected the younger girl for special attention, attacking her again and again throughout the night,' Justice Vincent said. 'To satisfy some drive within yourself, you subjected both of these victims to hours of terror and an ordeal which I suspect they appreciated from an early point of time they were almost certainly not going to survive.

'I consider your level of responsibility for the two murders to be great indeed, and at least equal to that of Beckett. I am satisfied that you gave the directions to kill, which Beckett had little difficulty in following.'

Justice Vincent then spoke about the unholy alliance of Camilleri and Beckett. 'Some reference should be made at this point to the nature of the association between the two of you, which was a curious one. I must confess that I am intrigued by the evidence that you were each unable to self-inject the amphetamine that you were both using quite regularly — and, it seems, only when you were together.

'This behaviour is even more curious in the light of the 1993 report tendered by your counsel which refers to a history of drug taking that included LSD, marijuana, cocaine and amphetamine. It suggests that your association with Beckett had become very close.

'There are clear parallels in your backgrounds, social attitudes and criminal propensities which enabled the development of strong bonds between you. I think that it would be a reasonable assessment of the situation to state that you both perceived yourselves as outcasts in a society which rejected you, and for the values and rules of which you had contempt.

'Tragically, you and Beckett found each other, and with your complementary personalities, formed an evil and deadly combination that potentiated the capacity for serious criminal behaviour in both of you.

'However, the sentence imposed upon Beckett was reduced in one important respect by reason of his plea of guilty and cooperating with the authorities. It is terrible to contemplate the prospect that as a consequence of the order which in my view justice and the proper application of sentencing principles would require in your case, you may never be released from prison. However, I consider that my duty is clear. Through your actions, you have forfeited your right to ever walk among us again. You are sentenced to imprisonment for life on each count, without the possibility of release on parole.'

Chapter 5

THE BUTCHER OF WOLLONGONG

Mark Mala Valera

On the morning of Saturday, 13 June 1998, the shockingly mutilated body of 59-year-old shopkeeper David John O'Hearn was discovered on the floor of the loungeroom at the townhouse where he lived alone at Albion Park, about 20 km southwest of Wollongong, the steelworkers' city on the coast about 90 km south of Sydney.

Police described the scene as 'gruesome in the extreme'. The dead man had been decapitated, and the head had been deposited in the kitchen sink. The left hand had been severed and was found on a sofa in the loungeroom. There were deep incisions to the abdomen, extending from just above the sternum down to the midpoint of the abdomen.

A post-mortem examination revealed five intersecting and parallel wounds on the lower chest. This wounding exposed the shaft of a hammer which had been inserted through the anus. The head of the hammer was visible between the buttocks of the deceased, who had been found with his jeans and underpants lowered to about the knee.

The deceased's penis had been mutilated and intestinal material had been disturbed. Near the foot of the body was a silver-coloured tray on which a section of intestine was resting. A number of sections of intestine were found lying on the breakfast bar in the kitchen.

On the floor near the deceased were a number of knives and other implements that had either been used to mutilate the body or placed there for that purpose. These items included a small metal saw, four knives, a razor blade and a corkscrew. There was a great deal of blood on the carpet near the body and there was blood splatter on items of furniture and curtains.

A blood-smeared wine decanter sat on a blood-stained lamp table, and the word 'Satan' had been written in blood on a mirror that was on the wall above the table. The same word had also been written in blood on the wall above the lounge suite upon which the severed hand was resting and immediately above that, also in blood, a pentagram — the five-pointed star used as a magical or occult symbol — had been drawn. On the wall beside the television set an inverted cross had been drawn in blood.

The post-mortem examination, conducted by Dr Cala, revealed that the mutilation of the body took place after death and that the head had been removed first. There were numerous lacerations to the scalp and a gross fracturing of the skull.

There was a deep Y-shaped laceration on the right side of the head with a grossly fractured section of skull underneath; Dr Cala found that the left eyeball had been depressed because the ball had been punctured by a sharp object.

Dr Cala said that in his opinion 10 to 12 blows would have been required to produce the lacerations he observed, and that there may have well been more blows that did not produce identifiable injuries. Extreme to severe force would have been needed to produce the head wounds, he said.

It was, in Dr Cala's opinion, the head injuries that caused death.

Police were mystified by David O'Hearn's brutal murder. From what they could establish, he was reclusive and lived alone, had no known enemies, had never been involved in any public scandals, and was most certainly not involved with the occult or associated with any groups that were.

Two weeks later, on 27 June, while police were still busy trying to get a handle on the O'Hearn murder, the body of Francis Neville Arkell was found at his home in Wollongong. Mr Arkell, 68, a former mayor of Wollongong, lived alone in a weatherboard house with an adjoining garage that he had converted into a granny flat.

Mr Arkell had been murdered in an attack very similar to the one made on David O'Hearn. So similar, in fact, that police had good reason to think that they may have a serial killer on their hands.

Wearing tracksuit pants and a white singlet, Mr Arkell was found lying on his back with his legs outstretched beside the bed in the granny flat. The flat was splattered with blood from wall to wall. The ceiling had been heavily sprayed with the victim's blood. The head of the deceased had been extensively traumatised and was resting in a large pool of blood.

Three tie pins had been placed in the victim's person — one in the left cheek, one in the corner of the left eye and one in the right eyelid — and there was a splinter of timber embedded in the neck. This had broken off a blood-soaked timber stake which was found on the bed.

There was a leather belt lying partially around the neck of the deceased, and the electrical cord of a lamp. Beside the bed was a broken timber lampstand which appeared to have been used in the attack. A glass ashtray was also used in the attack.

There was a lot of blood on the tiled floor of the bathroom, indicating that the deceased had been in that area when he was attacked. A pair of blood-soaked yellow Colorado hiking boots, Nike socks and black tracksuit pants — none of which turned out to belong to Mr Arkell — were found on the floor near the foot of the bed.

A post-mortem examination by Dr Cala revealed 34 injuries to the head region of the deceased. The teeth had been broken, and the hyoid bone and the sixth rib on the right had also been broken. The left jugular vein had been punctured.

In Dr Cala's opinion, Mr Arkell had died from the combined effect of both blunt and sharp force trauma to the neck, and strangulation.

Despite his brutal death, there were few tears shed for Frank Arkell. When news of his death spread through the district, the local talk was that if the police were looking for suspects, all they had to do was open the local telephone book at any page and pick a name.

Frank Arkell had been many things: an independent member of the New South Wales Legislative Assembly for several years, a wealthy local businessman, from a family of dairy farmers who had been granted land in the area in the last century, and a popular lord mayor — and the once cheery face behind the catch-cry of 'Wonderful Wollongong'.

For 17 years Frank Arkell had ruled Wollongong as though it was his own private property. He attended every birthday, wedding, football match and funeral that he could cram into his busy schedule. Every Thursday night Mr Arkell could be found out in the streets of his beloved city of 200,000, shaking hands and talking with every passer-by. His extraordinary memory for faces and names saw to it that he remembered them all, and he had a kind word for everyone.

Then Frank Arkell's world came crashing down around him. It had been rumoured for years that he was a predator of young boys in the district. These whispers saw to it that Mr Arkell lost his seat in 1991, and shortly after he was voted out as mayor.

On and off, over a period of several years, Mr Arkell had also been linked to a Wollongong paedophile ring — by 1998, he was alleged to be the last surviving member. The remainder of the group was said to have been another former mayor of Wollongong, Tony Bevan, who died of cancer in 1991 and was the alleged ring-leader; Brother Michael Evans, who was found dead in his car at Rockhampton, Queensland, in 1994, killed by carbon monoxide poisoning just as Wood Royal Commission investigators were looking to question him about child sex allegations; and former Wollongong councillor Brian William Tobin, 62, who also gassed himself in his car, in April 1996.

In 1994 Mr Arkell was named in the New South Wales Parliament by Deirdre Grusovin, MLC, as a paedophile. In 1996, it was alleged in the Wood Royal

Commission — which was looking into police corruption and whether or not police had covered up or failed to investigate allegations of paedophilia — that Mr Arkell had had sex with a 13-year-old boy in a Wollongong toilet block in the early 1970s after driving there in his mayoral car. It was also alleged that he had been given teenage boys for sex by his friend Tony Bevan.

At the time of his death Mr Arkell was on bail, awaiting trial on four charges involving the drugging and raping of two teenage boys. Mr Arkell had had 25 charges of sex offences thrown out of court the previous year at the committal hearing from which the drugging charges resulted.

In light of these allegations, it was little wonder that locals spat on Mr Arkell in the street. At the time of his death, someone had scrawled in large black graffiti across his brick front fence: 'W1 [this was Mr Arkell's code name in the Wood Royal Commission] you are a wanker.'

Mr Arkell was so despised by the media that two days after his murder, Sydney *Daily Telegraph* columnist Ray Chesterton wrote:

> However violently Frank Arkell might have died on Saturday at the hands of an unknown intruder, it was not enough. Not nearly enough. We can only hope those last fleeting seconds of his putrid life were as psychically painful as the mental and emotional torment he imposed on boys for a long time. Hopefully, as his life ebbed away, Arkell came to realise how depraved and debauched his life had been and suffered a moment of contrition.

Alex Mitchell, a senior reporter and columnist for the Sydney *Sun-Herald*, described Mr Arkell as a 'child-sex predator' and a 'practising paedophile with an insatiable appetite for boys' whose 'depraved tastes involved forcing sex on innocent boys as young as 10 and 12'.

The local paper, the *Illawarra Mercury*, which had openly campaigned against Mr Arkell and the other 'Gang of Four' members, produced an eight-page special titled 'The Arkell Murder Edition', in which it told of Mr Arkell's ambitions for Wollongong when he was lord mayor, and said that 'these civic duties pale into insignificance in comparison to the other dark side of his life'.

And now that he had the opportunity to speak out without fear of reprisal, a young man who was living interstate came forward and told of how he had been sexually abused by Mr Arkell — who was a trusted friend of his parents — from the age of 7, in the very room where Mr Arkell was found dead.

'It's so fitting and so ironic that he should be killed in the same flat that has given me such horrific memories,' the young man told the *Daily Telegraph*. 'I've been so happy all day since hearing about his death. I'm sure there's countless guys out there cheering with me today. In fact, there's a part of me that could have done it [murdered Arkell], and there's a part of me there when it happened.'

If police thought they would get a suspect from the crowd at Frank Arkell's funeral, they were to be disappointed: only a dozen men and women turned up at the family tomb for the burial, and every one of them could be accounted for at the time of the murder. They were conspicuous only because they were at the service.

Over the ensuing weeks, more young men came forward with stories of abuse at the hands of Frank Arkell. And allegations were rife that Mr Arkell and his paedophile associates could only have operated for as long as they had because the police turned a blind eye to them and their activities. But they were only allegations. And nothing came of them.

Three months after Frank Arkell's body was discovered, 19-year-old former Planet Hollywood dishwasher Mark Mala Valera walked into the Wollongong police station and confessed to murdering both men. Valera said that he had decided to give himself up because it 'seemed like the right thing to do'.

He told police that he had never met David O'Hearn before, that on the day he killed him he 'just wanted someone to kill', and that he went to Mr O'Hearn's house 'just random'. He said that there was no forward planning; he just felt angry and felt he 'could kill someone'.

In his statement, Valera said that he gained access to Mr O'Hearn's townhouse on the pretext that he was looking for somewhere to live: 'I stayed at the door and asked if there was any, like ... accommodation around,' he said, 'and the bloke said, "Come in and we'll talk about it."'

Valera used the term 'just random' on numerous occasions, and told police that he had confessed the crimes to his martial arts teacher just before coming in to give himself up. He told police that he had counted the number of times he had struck Mr O'Hearn over the head with the decanter. He said that he hit Mr

O'Hearn 10 times and then concluded that he was dead because he had no pulse.

According to Valera, he next went upstairs looking for valuables, then returned downstairs and rounded up the instruments he needed — knives, a hacksaw, a corkscrew and a hammer — to dissect Mr O'Hearn's body. He then proceeded to mutilate the body, after which he used the severed hand to draw the pentagram on the wall in the victim's blood.

Valera repeated that he had no reason to murder Mr O'Hearn; it was just that on the night he felt angry and had to kill someone.

The murder of Frank Arkell was a different story. Valera told police that he knew of Mr Arkell and that he was a 'very, very horrible man'. Valera said that he went to the deceased's home because he had made up his mind that he wanted to kill him. He said that he went there under false pretences: he had rung Mr Arkell up, telling him he (Valera) was gay, and had invited himself to Mr Arkell's house.

Valera repeated many times that he went to Mr Arkell's house specifically to kill him, and that after having spoken to Mr Arkell for only a couple of minutes, he attacked him. Valera said that he picked up the lamp and hit Mr Arkell around the head with it about 40 times. He said that Mr Arkell tried to get away by crawling across the floor, but that he caught him and used a lamp cord to strangle him.

Valera told police that when he thought that Mr Arkell was dead he kicked him in the face a number of times and then pushed the three tie pins into his face. Then he tried to push a garden fork into Mr Arkell's neck but the wooden handle broke off.

Valera left his bloodied Colorado boots and tracksuit pants at the murder scene and wore a pair of his victim's tracksuit pants when he left. Valera said that he didn't like his victim because of 'all the nasty things he has done to kids. Read about him. Heard about him in the papers and the media.'

'I knew of him, I knew he was a paedophile,' he said. 'I knew it wasn't for me to take it into my hands but ... I felt someone should've killed him [for] all the nasty things he's done to those kids.'

When police searched Valera's Wollongong unit, they found a copy of *The A–Z Encyclopedia of Serial Killers* which had the words 'Who will be my number three?' and 'The first one is always the best' scrawled across its pages.

Beneath were listed the names of Mr Arkell and Mr O'Hearn and a request for 'volunteers' for a third victim. Police also found a handwritten poem titled 'Scattered Remains, Splattered Brains' about a 'psychotic coroner' and 'slicing' people up and cutting out their eyes.

Valera was charged with the murders of Frank Arkell and David O'Hearn. In May 1999, when he was committed for trial, the prosecutor, Ray Willis, took the unusual step of addressing the media in order to make it perfectly clear that Mr O'Hearn was in no way connected to Mr Arkell or Mr Arkell's sexual preferences.

'The selection of David O'Hearn [as a victim] was an entirely random thing,' Mr Willis said. '[His] murder was not motivated by any sexual orientation he may have had, and indeed the defendant denied any knowledge of [O'Hearn's] sexual orientation.

'Apart from the fact that the prosecution alleges that the defendant killed both men, there is no evidence that there was any connection between the murders, nor that there was any connection between the two deceased.'

At his trial, which began in the New South Wales Supreme Court in Wollongong on 12 July 2000 before Justice Timothy Studdart, Mark Valera, also known as Mark Van Krevel, pleaded not guilty to murder but guilty on two counts of manslaughter.

Valera's defence counsel, John Nicholson, said that his client suffered post-traumatic stress caused by years of alleged physical, mental and sexual abuse by his 44-year-old father, Jack Van Krevel, and that when Valera committed the murders, he was convinced that it was his abusive father he was killing.

Mr Nicholson said his client was suffering from a 'substantial impairment', and/or he lost control because of the conduct of the deceased. Mr Nicholson told the court that Valera lost control when each of the men asked him (Valera) to be the 'active partner' in anal sex.

Mr Nicholson said that there were three forces working on Valera at the time of the killings: anger and frustration, which he felt when having to deal with homosexuality; loathing for his father, Jack Van Krevel, whom he alleged had physically and sexually abused him since he was 7; and his interest in — and the impact of — 'things satanic'.

The court heard that the prisoner was born Mark Van Krevel on 24 April 1979. His mother left home when he was 2 or 3 years old. His earliest memory of his father being violent to him was at the age of about 6 or 7, when he was thrown into a toy box. On

It is no secret that Paul Steven Haigh desperately wanted to be remembered as Victoria's worst mass murderer. He almost succeeded. Among his seven victims were a woman and her 9-year-old son, two citizens going about their business, and a prison inmate.

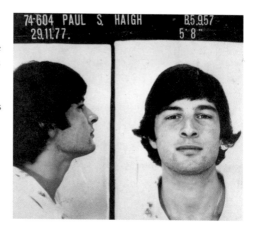

As a 14-year-old schoolboy, Ashley Coulston kidnapped two teachers at gunpoint. In 1989 he became a hero when he sailed a spa-bath sized yacht to New Zealand and back. He is in jail forever for the execution-style murders of three strangers. PHOTO NEWSPIX

When first confronted about the murders of two schoolgirls, Paul Osborne denied any knowledge. When told his wallet was found at the murder scene, Osborne confessed saying: 'I hit them and hit them. I don't know why. They seemed pretty nice.' PHOTO NEWSPIX

Out on bail on a technicality, Leslie Camilleri, a drug-addled bully with a record of 146 convictions, could have been serving a lengthy jail term for child sex offences when he and Lindsay Beckett murdered two schoolgirls. PHOTO NEWSPIX

Something snapped in Mark Valera and he murdered and mutilated two men in horrendous circumstances. While Valera was in jail serving life for the murders, Valera's father was murdered in similar fashion.

PHOTO CHRIS HYDE, NEWSPIX

When his car stopped at the lights, gun-totin' gangster Michael Kanaan shot dead two strangers fighting outside a Sydney hotel. Then Kanaan and other members of his gang murdered their boss to take over his drug distribution empire. It didn't work.

PHOTO BILL COUNSELL, NEWSPIX

Bandali Debs (right) and Jason Roberts (left) were a couple of armed hold-up specialists when they bumped into two police officers on a stake-out. Rather than try and escape, they chose to execute the policemen.

PHOTO TREVOR PINDER, NEWSPIX

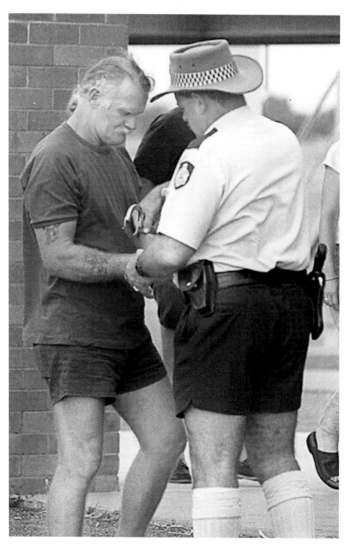

Leonard Fraser was already serving life imprisonment for child murder when he was charged with the serial murders of four women. The case caused an uproar when one of his alleged victims turned up alive and well during the trial. PHOTO NEWSPIX

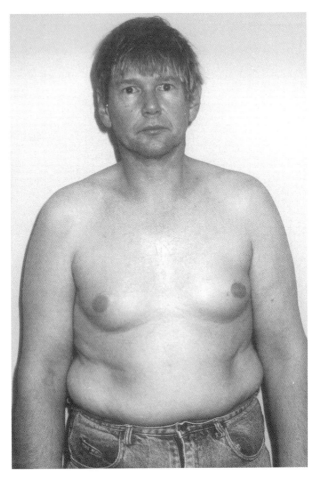

All of his life, serial rapist Peter Norris Dupas re-offended within a short time of being released from prison. Each time his crimes became worse. It was only a matter of time before he committed a horrific murder.

Mother, housewife and abattoir worker Katherine Knight kept her boning knives above her bed. She skinned her de-facto husband John Price (in picture) and then hung his pelt in the doorway. She then cut off his head and served up parts of his body for his children's dinner. PHOTO NEWSPIX

Super Max, the impenetrable fortress that is home to some of Australia's worst prisoners.

PHOTO BEN KIDD

A cell in Super Max looking back into the small adjoining courtyard.

PHOTO BEN KIDD

The duty officer checks on a prisoner at the induction centre where incoming Super Max inmates are processed. PHOTO BEN KIDD

another occasion he had had a loaded rifle held to his head and was told by his father that he was about to have his brains blown out. The prisoner wet himself on that occasion and on many other occasions for fear of what his father was going to do to him.

Mr Nicholson told the court that, as a boy, the defendant was frequently kicked and punched by his father. This happened a few times a week until he was 15 years of age. Thereafter the frequency of any physical violence diminished; the last time his father was violent to him was when he was aged 17, when his father punched him in the face and he had to go to hospital.

The court also heard the defendant claim that his father started sexually abusing him when he was 7 years of age. The initial abuse took the form of the father fondling his son's penis and putting his finger in the boy's anus. The boy and his father had mutual oral sex and the boy was forced to masturbate his father.

Mr Nicholson alleged that from then on his client was sexually assaulted by his father on a regular basis. These assaults included his father forcing anal intercourse upon him and forcing him to masturbate him and 'suck him off'. Over a period of four years, his father forced anal intercourse upon him at least 20 times. Once, when he was 12, he was forced to perform anal intercourse on his father.

Mr Nicholson said that at age 18 his client had left home to get away from his father. He went to live with his schoolfriend, Keith Andrew Schreiber. He changed his name to Valera from Van Krevel by deed poll.

In the witness box, Mark Valera told the court that he had lied in his earlier statement to police: he did in fact know Frank Arkell, and for more than a year he had been Mr Arkell's casual lover. He told the jury that on the night that he killed Mr Arkell he was 'put on the spot' when the former Wollongong mayor asked him to be the active partner in sex. Valera said that Mr Arkell's request reminded him of his father.

Valera told the jury that his other victim, David O'Hearn, whom he killed two weeks before Mr Arkell, had made a similar request. Valera claimed that he did in fact also know Mr O'Hearn: he had gone to Mr O'Hearn's Dapto shop on 12 June 1998, and Mr O'Hearn masturbated him in a closet.

Valera alleged that Mr O'Hearn had invited him to his home that evening. He arrived at about 6 pm and they started to watch pornographic movies. After about 15 minutes, he said that Mr O'Hearn got on the floor and asked Valera to have sex with him.

'That's when I grabbed the wine decanter and whacked him over the head with it,' Valera told the jury. 'I felt like I was put right on the spot and I was there and there was no way out of it.'

Mark Valera's father, Jack Van Krevel, took the stand and told the court that he worked locally as a carpenter and was a violent man with a bad temper. Mr Van Krevel acknowledged that he had been guilty of physical attacks upon his son; he explained his behaviour was a result of, a response to, his wife having left the family. He said that he had hit and punched his son and kicked him — both when he was standing up and when he was on the ground.

Mr Van Krevel admitted throwing a spanner at his son on one occasion, intending to hit him with it, and abusing him verbally, including teasing him about his slow speech.

But while he freely admitted physical abuse to his son, Mr Van Krevel vehemently denied, throughout a testing cross-examination, that he had ever sexually assaulted his son.

Mark Valera's sister, Belinda Van Krevel, who was 18 months older than her brother, told the court that while she didn't actually observe any act of physical abuse to her brother, when she was 13 years of age her father would read her to sleep while wearing nothing but his dressing gown, and that he would frequently go down the hall and into her brother's bedroom and then close the door. She said that that had occurred from the time she was 13 onwards.

The prosecutor, Paul Conlon, told the court about a conversation allegedly overheard by a Crown witness, in which Mark Valera said that his father would be his third victim.

'Dad is number three,' Valera allegedly said. 'I haven't finished my journey yet.'

On 8 August 2000 Mark Valera was found guilty of the murders of David O'Hearn and Frank Arkell. His sentence was to be handed down on 21 December 2000. As Valera was being taken away, his mother, Ms Elizabeth Carroll, who had attended the proceedings from day one, broke down and sobbed loudly.

'That's my son,' she cried out, becoming increasingly distressed. 'I gave birth to him. It's not fair. His father did this to him.'

'Don't worry about it,' Valera responded, as he was led from the court. 'Paedophiles always get away with it.'

If police thought that the conviction of Mark Valera was the final chapter in the Wollongong horrors, they were very much mistaken. On 18 August, 10 days after his son had been convicted of double murder, the mutilated body of Mark Valera's father, Jack Van Krevel, was found in his home. Mr Van Krevel had been butchered almost beyond recognition: he'd been stabbed from head to foot, chopped up with an axe, and his head had been almost severed.

Later that day, Valera's flatmate, Keith Schreiber, 21, turned himself into police and confessed to the murder of Jack Van Krevel. Schreiber was no stranger to police and local mental health care units. He had a juvenile record for holding up the Albion Park Rail service station with a samurai sword.

Schreiber was described as having low self-esteem as a result of being bullied and neglected over many years. He had a fascination with Satan and had been described in Mark Valera's trial as a devil worshipper. The Illawarra mobile mental health crisis team had interviewed Schreiber after he had complained to them of suicidal and homicidal thoughts.

Schreiber had said then that his flatmate, Mark Valera, had been jailed for murder and that he himself had nowhere to live and was 'stressed out'. He was offered voluntary admission to a psychiatric unit but rejected the offer; he said that he didn't have any immediate plans to kill anyone and was allowed to go.

Three days later Belinda Van Krevel turned up at the local police station at 3 am saying that she had just found her father dead. It was later the same day that Schreiber walked into the police station and confessed to the killing.

For a man who was allegedly such a monster, there was a large turnout at Jack Van Krevel's funeral, which was held at the Lakeside Crematorium Chapel at Dapto, south of Wollongong. At the service, family and friends spoke of Jack's good nature and kindness, and all agreed that he adored his two children and would never harm them, let alone sexually assault them. To those who had known him all his life, it was simply out of the question.

The general consensus of the group was that their deceased friend took the stand at the trial and admitted to bashing his son in the belief that agreeing with Valera's story of paternal abuse might help his boy get a lighter sentence. The mourners saw their friend off in the belief that he was a good and decent man who had been the victim of a horrific injustice.

At his committal hearing, held on 28 November 2000 at the Wollongong Local Court, Keith Andrew Schreiber pleaded not guilty to the murder of Jack Van Krevel. However, in a police record of interview tendered in court, Schreiber said that he had killed Mr Van Krevel to revenge his friend Mark Valera and Valera's sister, Belinda.

The police brief also alleged that four days before he was killed, the late Mr Van Krevel was told by his ex-wife, Elizabeth Carroll, that their daughter, Belinda, had hired Schreiber to kill him. Ms Carroll said that Belinda was paying Schreiber out of her dole payments, and that when she got to $32,000 he was going to kill Jack Van Krevel.

The court heard that in the police interview Schreiber described how he hacked into Mr Van Krevel with a tomahawk while he slept and then attacked him with a knife and tried to cut his heart out. Schreiber also told police that while Mr Van Krevel was still alive and in a kneeling position he (Schreiber) left the bedroom and got a poker from the loungeroom fire, then returned and hit Mr Krevel with it repeatedly, until he heard Mr Van Krevel's backbone break.

Keith Schreiber was committed for trial for the murder of Jack Van Krevel.

At Mark Valera's sentencing for the murders of David O'Hearn and Frank Arkell, on 21 December 2000 in the New South Wales Supreme Court, Justice Timothy Studdart said during his summing up:

'David O'Hearn was subjected to the most savage attack, and I am satisfied beyond reasonable doubt that the prisoner acted in such attack with intent to kill and that it was a random and utterly senseless killing.

'The way in which the prisoner mutilated the body of this victim showed his utter contempt for his victim and so too did his use of the severed hand and his writings on the wall and on the mirror. Indeed, this first crime scene exuded evil of the prisoner's making.

'Francis Arkell was likewise subjected to the most brutal attack, and again I am satisfied beyond reasonable doubt that the prisoner conducted the attack with intent to kill. The prisoner sought to explain, and indeed to justify, his attack upon an adverse judgment he had formed of his second victim.'

Justice Studdart sentenced Mark Mala Valera to two terms of life imprisonment without the possibility of parole. This made Valera the third-youngest prisoner ever to be sent to jail in Australia for life without parole. The others were 14-year-old Bronson Blessington and 16-year-old Matthew Elliott, for the abduction, rape and murder of 21-year-old bank clerk Janine Balding in 1988.

At his trial on 1 March 2001, Keith Andrew Schreiber changed his plea, this time pleading guilty to the murder of Jack Van Krevel. He told the court that after climbing in through a window left open for him by his lover, Belinda Van Krevel, he crept into Jack's room and began to attack him.

Schreiber told the court that Jack recognised him and called out 'Keith' as he (Schreiber) began to 'deliver him' and 'assist his destiny' by stabbing him more than 50 times in his head, neck and torso.

'I just wanted it to be quick ... [I said] "Die, you fucker, hurry up and fucking die,"' Schreiber said. 'He [Van Krevel] rolled off and was going "Hey, hey, hey" ... I got him a few more times ... the fucking prick wouldn't die ... resilient bastard.

'I said to him: "This is from Mark, you fucking paedophile bastard. You'll never molest kids again."'

Schreiber told the court that he and Mark Van Krevel had met at school and had become firm friends because they had similar tastes in satanism, death and dismemberment. When they shared a flat, they spent most of their time talking about death.

Keith Schreiber was found guilty of the murder of Jack Van Krevel. On 11 May 2001, at his sentencing hearing, the court heard that Belinda Van Krevel may indeed have solicited Schreiber to kill her father.

The court was told that the day before Mr Van Krevel's murder, Schreiber had spent several hours shopping with Ms Van Krevel, and had bought a pair of black woollen gloves which he used during the killing.

On 1 June 2001, 20-year-old Belinda Van Krevel was charged with the murder of her father. At her committal hearing the Wollongong Local Court was told that Van Krevel, a single mother with a $1000 a week drug habit, had gone to 'extreme lengths' to interfere with the police investigation into the murder of her father.

A police statement said that these extreme lengths included death threats, soliciting others to kill or harm witnesses, and intimidation. Police alleged that Van Krevel had a deep hatred for her father and had asked several people to kill him. In the days before his death, Mr Van Krevel told others that he had discovered that his daughter had taken out a contract on his life.

Van Krevel was living with her father at the time of his death and was the person who raised the alarm, telling the police that she had heard noises like someone being murdered coming from his bedroom. Van Krevel alleged that after the murdering noises ceased, Schreiber — who was also her lover — covered in blood, opened her bedroom door and said, 'Hey, babe, it's finished.'

A police statement read out in court said that electronic surveillance and witness statements had identified the accused offering persons $2000 and a car to have witnesses, and her mother, Ms Carroll, murdered or seriously injured in an attempt to prevent them speaking in court about their knowledge of her involvement in her father's murder.

Van Krevel was committed for trial on charges of murder and soliciting Keith Schreiber to commit murder.

At Keith Schreiber's sentencing, in the New South Wales Supreme Court on 19 December 2001, Justice Peter Hidden said that the defendant's life was a pitiful lot. Schreiber had been sexually assaulted by a teacher in primary school and blamed himself for his parents divorcing when he was 12. When both his parents remarried he was made unwelcome by both his new step-parents.

Justice Hidden said that Schreiber had become increasingly dependent on his friendship with Valera and Valera's sister, Belinda Van Krevel, and that Van Krevel had been 'a malign influence on him'.

'Whatever her role might have been, I am satisfied that to a significant degree the offender's actions were the result of her influence,' Justice Hidden said. Keith Schreiber was sentenced to 16 years in jail with a 12-year non-parole period for the murder of Jack Van Krevel.

At her trial for murder and soliciting Keith Schreiber to commit murder, held at the Sydney Supreme Court on 23 July 2002, Belinda Van Krevel pleaded not guilty to all charges.

Van Krevel told the court that she and her daughter were woken during the early hours by the sound of someone repeatedly striking Jack Van Krevel about the head and neck with a tomahawk. She said that she heard moaning and groaning, and her daughter asked her: 'What's happening? What's happening? Poppy! Poppy!'

Van Krevel said that when the noises stopped Schreiber came into her bedroom, leaving a bloody handprint on the door, and told her that her father was dead. Then Schreiber, Van Krevel and her three-year-old daughter watched TV and ate vegemite sandwiches.

When she arrived at the police station to report the murder, Ms Van Krevel had told police that she thought her father had been killed by an intruder.

The prosecution was quick to point out that despite having a mobile phone in the bedroom, Van Krevel didn't raise the alarm at any time during the attack, although it had taken her lover over an hour to hack her father to death.

Van Krevel eventually pleaded guilty to the lesser charge of soliciting the murder, and on 4 April 2003 was sentenced to six years' imprisonment, with a non-parole period of four years.

Belinda Van Krevel will be eligible for parole in May 2005. Keith Andrew Schreiber will be eligible for parole in August 2012.

Mark Mala Valera is never to be released.

Chapter 6

THE STONE KILLER

Michael Kanaan

Michael Kanaan executed three men in cold blood. Two of his victims were young men fighting outside the front of a suburban hotel in Sydney. Both were complete strangers to him.

Kanaan's other victim was his rapacious employer, crime boss Danny Karam, who had been ripping Kanaan off for the bulk of the profits from the lucrative Kings Cross street drug trade, which Karam controlled through his gang of thugs and dealers known as 'DK's Boys'. Led by Kanaan, DK's Boys murdered their boss in a send-off that any capo with a use-by date would have been proud of.

An unlikely gangster, Michael Kanaan was born in 1975 into a loving and respectable family and was educated at the highly regarded Christian Brothers school in Lewisham, in Sydney's inner west. The polite, well-spoken and respectful young man went on to university for two years and unsuccessfully applied to join the Australian Federal Police.

Then, for no apparent reason, Michael Kanaan went from a conscientious student and useful football player to a minor felon, with convictions for drug possession and assault, to a multiple murderer — all in a matter of a few drug-hazed years.

Tired of life in his working-class neighbourhood of Canterbury Bankstown, with its high unemployment and even higher crime rate, it wasn't long before Kanaan was making the regular 40-minute pilgrimage to the bright lights of Kings Cross and the drugs and other temptations that went with them.

Unafraid to use a knife, fists, a club or a gun, by the time he was 22 Kanaan had endeared himself to Kings Cross drug boss Danny Karam, and was putting his talents to good use on the streets, collecting protection money for his employer.

Karam's formula was as old as organised crime itself. He had a prime area on the Kings Cross strip that he guarded from intruders with threats of bashings or worse; anyone who wanted to trade within that area paid him for the privilege. The only overheads Karam had were paying off the crooked cops who saw to it that his problems were minimal.

Street dealers or 'runners' — mainly teenage kids fresh out of school, easily identified by their uniform of designer label tracksuits and runners — paid $1000 a head each Sunday night to use Karam's territory without fear of reprisals for a week or part thereof.

They sold painkiller capsules or 'caps' filled with heroin or cocaine, usually for around $60 to $80, depending on the customer or how tough the competition was. They kept these caps in their mouths in individual miniature balloons that they could swallow in the rare event of being picked up by the police.

Once the runners had sold their supply they would return to their main dealer, who conducted business from a private hotel room or apartment nearby. The runners paid their dealer between $40 and $60 per cap and pocketed the rest. Each time they settled their account they would be given more caps, and off they would go again.

Depending on product availability and competition, the teenage salesmen on Danny Karam's strip could collectively pay as little as $5000 or as much as $28,000 a week in rent to Kanaan and his sidekick, 23-year-old tough guy Alan Rossini (Rossini is an alias stipulated by the court when this man became a police informer), who kicked the lot upstairs to their boss.

If a dealer was late with the rent — or, heaven forbid, didn't pay at all — there would be punishment. The punishment would vary, depending on the gravity of the unfortunate's misdemeanour, from a savage beating to a bullet through the back of the kneecap as an example to the others.

Born in Lebanon in 1962, Danny Karam immigrated to Australia in 1977, and by the time he hit the Cross, in the early 1980s, he was a career criminal, with a stretch in Long Bay and a heroin habit to his credit. Karam could fight like a threshing machine, and kept his body toned and fit. He carried a gun and was partial to using it.

Karam made his way up through the ranks as a minder for the heavyweight Kings Cross drug traffickers, learning the business as he went, and then climbed over their bodies as they were either killed or sent to prison.

By 1997 Danny Karam was one of the four major drug bosses of Kings Cross — last in the pecking order, but still moving up.

Now, while Danny Karam had good organising skills, he lacked generosity, and it was this that would ultimately bring about his demise at the hands of his own trusted minions. And from all accounts he had made so many enemies on his rise to the top of the cesspool that if it hadn't been his own gang, it could have been any one of a countless number of other enemies.

The tall, muscular Rossini was recruited as an enforcer by Danny Karam in 1997. A few years earlier, Rossini had formed a friendship with Michael Kanaan, the common denominator being that both their parents had emigrated from Lebanon. They spent most of their time hanging out together kickboxing at the gym and smoking pot. Rossini soon introduced Kanaan to DK (as Danny Karam preferred to be called), and in a matter of weeks the two of them were installed as the boss's minders. The trio became inseparable.

Rossini and Kanaan did everything for DK, from buying his personal heroin, cocaine and guns to picking up his dry-cleaning and filling his car with petrol. They were always on call, and when they met they would embrace and kiss in the manner of Mafia gangsters. DK thought so much of his 'Boys' that he had elaborate gold rings made up for each of them: Kanaan's was stamped with an M for Michael, Rossini's with an A for Alan, and his own with a K.

But that's as far as DK's generosity went. While he was pulling in thousands of dollars each week, he was paying his Boys a pittance, sometimes only a few hundred dollars a week, telling them that their share was being put aside; he was 'looking after it' for them.

In order to provide for their own extravagances — cocaine, new guns and the clothes that would make them look the part — DK's Boys set up their own dealers. These dealers would sell what were in fact the Boys' caps on their usual territory, then pay rent back to the Boys, expecting it to go straight to the boss. The Boys would give the dealers a small percentage and keep all the profits, bypassing the boss altogether. While it might seem a hard way to make a buck, it earned them in the vicinity of $5000 a week each.

On the night of Friday, 17 July 1998, Rossini, Kanaan and three associates were driving along Great Northern Road, in Sydney's inner west, when they saw three men in an altercation outside the Five Dock Hotel.

They stopped the car and words were exchanged. Kanaan got out of the car with his .22 pistol in his hand and shot 25-year-old Michael Hurle in the chest, 23-year-old Adam Wright in the lower abdomen and 38-year-old Ronald Singleton in the shoulder. Hurle and Wright, both promising footballers, died. Singleton survived.

Well away from the murder scene, Kanaan and his cohorts dumped the car, which was registered to an associate, to make it appear that it had been stolen — in case anyone had written down the numberplate. No one had. Police investigators were left without a positive lead.

Kanaan dyed his short black hair blond, and he and Rossini disappeared from the Sydney scene and went to the south coast for a few weeks. When he thought it was safe to come back to town he resumed his work with Danny Karam as if nothing had happened. What the boss thought of his two gofers' disappearance or whether or not they told him of their involvement in the killings isn't clear.

In the winter of 1998 Kanaan, Rossini and another three of DK's Boys, Wassim El-Assaad, Rabeeh Mawas and Charlie Gea Gea, set up a 'safe house' on the first floor of the exclusive Addison Apartments in Riley Street, Surry Hills, a five-minute drive from Kings Cross. Here they stashed their mounting arsenal, and spent their time watching gangster videos, bonging marijuana and 'capping' and snorting cocaine.

They all agreed that they were being ripped off by their boss and that it was only a matter of time before he would have to go and they would take over his empire. But while the nuts and bolts of the assassination were being put together, it was business as usual.

Meanwhile, a rival gang was trying to take over Danny Karam's turf. He summoned his troops to give them a warning. On the night of 11 September 1998, several gunmen in two cruising cars shot up the EPI Nightclub, spraying over 40 bullets into the front of the building, sending doormen and patrons ducking for cover. The EPI was owned by the Ibrahim brothers, Sam and John, past employers of Danny Karam. Police arrived within minutes but the shooters had long gone.

Just after 1 am on 1 November 1998, the Lakemba police station in Sydney's southwest was blasted with gunfire — 17 bullets were fired into the doors and windows at the front of the building, but luckily no police officers or civilians were hit. DK's Boys were showing support for a local gang of stolen car 're-birthers' the cops had been too interested in.

While the shooting-up of a police station was unheard of in Sydney until then, and the Police Commissioner, Peter Ryan, was outraged, an increasingly nervous public was starting to feel that gang violence was getting out of hand and that some criminals thought themselves untouchable.

On 11 November 1998 gunmen opened fire on homes in Eveleigh Street, the main residential street in the predominantly Aboriginal area of the inner-city suburb of Redfern. Miraculously, no one was hit, though 15 homes were damaged. The shooters left behind an Aboriginal flag on which was printed: 'FUCK WITH OUR BROTHERS INSIDE WE FUCK WITH YOUR FAMILIES OUTSIDE. BLOOD 4 BLOOD. LITHGOW JAIL 2 DIE 4.'

It turned out later that the Redfern shoot-up was a reprisal for an attack on an associate of DK's Boys (in Lithgow Prison) by an Aboriginal inmate. But at the time the police didn't know the details. Instead they pondered this sudden outbreak of violence, the likes of which Sydney had never seen before: the mysterious murders of the two men at Five Dock, the shoot-up at Kings Cross, the attack on the Lakemba police station, scores of kneecappings within the drug industry and now the apparently unprovoked assault on inner-city residences, all within the space of five months. Decisive action was needed.

Commissioner Ryan formed a special strike force, which eventually became known as Mask. In stating the obvious, the Commissioner said that the growing incidence of guns being used to settle disputes and shoot at police was outrageous and would not be tolerated. The public agreed and wondered when they would see some results. The results did come, but only after another violent murder and a shoot-out with the police.

By December 1998 the conspiracy to murder Danny Karam was at the stage where DK's Boys were discussing methods of dispatch and venues for the event. They had decided that he would have to be shot.

On the night of 13 December 1998, Danny Karam was hit with 17 bullets from three different guns as he sat in his car in Surry Hills. He died instantly.

Word of Karam's assassination spread through the Cross like a bushfire fanned by gale-force winds, and that night his rivals took over a nightclub and celebrated the good news late into the morning. Now unsure of who they had to pay rent to for the use of DK's turf, the dealers gave his turf a wide berth for fear of a hiding from his thugs, who might well be seeking revenge.

While at first there was suspicion that another gang had murdered Danny Karam, in the kind of gangland grab for territory that had been going on since gang wars were invented, a few whispers in the right ears had police deciding to ask DK's Boys about their whereabouts at the time their boss got whacked.

In an attempt to throw police off their tails, Kanaan and his crew decided to take out the top enforcer in a rival gang as 'revenge' for their boss's murder. They hoped this would send the investigators off in some other direction.

The tension in the Cross was like a festering carbuncle about to burst. And 10 days after the death of Danny Karam it erupted, but not in the manner that anyone had expected.

At 3 am on Wednesday, 23 December 1998, Rossini, Kanaan, El-Assaad and another gang member were trawling the streets of the Cross in a car loaded up with pistols and semi-automatic rifles in search of members of the Ibrahim Brothers' gang — their rivals. Their main target was the gang's chief enforcer, 'Tongan' Sam Ngata.

Two alert constables in a cruiser, John Fotopoulos and Chris Patrech, became suspicious of the vehicle and its passengers, and as they unhurriedly turned their patrol car around to check out the situation, the car screeched off in the direction of the eastern suburbs. The officers gave chase.

The Boys careered down Bayswater Road into Rushcutters Bay on the edge of the Cross, took a sharp right through the traffic lights into Neild Avenue, gathered momentum on the straight then took a left into Lawson Street and then another sharp left into Alma Street — and wound up facing a dead-end: the wire fence at the Weigall Sports Ground and the gates to the White City Tennis Club.

Grabbing their pistols, the Boys took to the ground running. They scaled the wire mesh fence with the two constables a few breaths behind them and the wailing of the back-up they had called for growing louder by the second.

In the gun battle that followed in the Weigall Sports Ground, officer Patrech was shot twice and wounded; El-Assaad was shot and wounded in the back while running away; Kanaan was wounded seven times, smashing the bones in his legs; Rossini dropped his gun and threw his hands in the air; and the fourth gang member escaped into suburban Paddington, much to the horror of the suburb's middle-class residents, who were woken in the middle of the night by the ensuing police dragnet.

At bedside court hearings the following day — Christmas Eve — El-Assaad was granted bail on the condition that he did not contact Constable Patrech or his family or those related to the other officer involved. He was charged with possession of ammunition.

Kanaan, who was unable to walk because of the wounds to his legs, was charged with two counts of shooting with intent to murder, one count of shooting to avoid lawful apprehension, one count of possessing an unlicensed pistol, one count of discharging a firearm in a public place and one count of possessing a loaded firearm in a public place. He did not apply for bail and was remanded in custody.

Kanaan was confined to a wheelchair for some time; he was eventually released on bail. On 2 June 1999, he was back on the front pages: he staged a siege by locking himself and five other people in his Belfield home when police attempted to raid the premises for drugs. Kanaan told the press that he had already been shot 'nine times' by the police and he feared that officers would kill him if he let them into his home.

After two days, and only when the television cameras were outside his house, Kanaan came out. The following day he appeared in the Liverpool Local Court and was charged with conspiring to supply a commercial quantity of cocaine. He was refused bail.

At Kanaan's hearing for the charges incurred during the Rushcutters Bay shoot-out, it was revealed to the court that Police Constable John Fotopoulos had tested positive to marijuana after the event. Magistrate Pat

O'Shane also noted that there were 'very significant discrepancies' between the two officers' statements.

Magistrate O'Shane said that there was no evidence that police had a lawful reason to arrest Michael Kanaan before he allegedly opened fire on them. 'There is not a shred of evidence that any of these police officers had any reason to suspect the accused of having committed a felony,' she said. Magistrate O'Shane also said that Sydney police in particular had a long history of chasing and harassing young people.

The court was told that the police started shooting first and that Constable Patrech was hit in the wrist and the knee as he scaled the wire fence to pursue the men who had fled from the car. Constable Patrech then told the court that he had described the incident as 'like 300 times an orgasm'.

The court also heard that a CZ model 75 9 mm pistol was found near Kanaan after he was injured. It was alleged that he had fired it at the police. Constable Patrech gave evidence that Kanaan was the shooter but Ms O'Shane said his account of the events differed from that of another witness. The ballistics evidence was unable to prove which gun had fired the shots that caused the injuries to Constable Patrech. In all, 20 shots were fired.

On 29 November 1999, Sydneysiders watching the evening news heard that not only had the main shooter in the Rushcutters Bay gun battle with the police, Michael Kanaan, been exonerated, but instead of being recommended for bravery awards, the two constables involved had been severely berated by the magistrate for being 'stupid, reckless and foolhardy' in their actions.

Magistrate O'Shane had also attacked police training methods and recommended that young officers be warned on the dangers of 'reckless bravado'.

'Fotopoulos was the driver of the police vehicle on the night, and for no cause gave chase to Kanaan and his cohorts,' Magistrate O'Shane said. 'When their vehicle came to a stop, and they decamped, both officers gave chase to the men. That was stupid, reckless and foolhardy. Even had the shooting not taken place, it was dark, and deserted, and there were three men that they knew of.

'There was nothing which called for such behaviour. Had they exercised the caution that society might expect of well-trained, cool-headed police officers, then they would have stopped at the abandoned vehicle and checked it out. It is hoped that police training will include advice, to young officers in particular, about the dangers of foolhardy and reckless behaviour. This case is an object lesson.

'Society has a right to expect a professional law enforcement service. We need to protect good officers, and encourage them in their necessary duty,' she said. Ms O'Shane also said that despite the fact that it was later discovered that the men were armed on the night, 'The end does not justify the means.'

The police, much of the public, and the officers' families were outraged. The Police Association immediately called for a review of the case by the Director of Public Prosecutions (DPP). The director, Nicholas Cowdery, said he would look into the matter immediately.

On 15 December 1999, the DPP overturned Magistrate O'Shane's controversial decision and ordered

Kanaan, who was still in custody on the cocaine charges, to stand trial early the following year on the charges arising from the Rushcutters Bay incident.

But by then the charges arising from the incident at Rushcutters Bay were the least of Michael Kanaan's worries. In the meantime, to save his own skin on a number of cocaine trafficking charges, Rossini had done a back-flip and was 'ratting' on his mates to the New South Wales Crime Commission about the drive-by shooting-up of the Lakemba police station, a shooting at Gladesville, the Five Dock murders and 'other things' that DK's Boys had been up to.

The investigators were especially interested in the Five Dock murders, and their new star witness was more than happy to tell all he knew — in return for complete immunity.

In February 2001, Michael Kanaan found himself in the dock of the Sydney Supreme Court before Mr Justice Greg James, charged with two murders. The chief witness against him was — surprise, surprise — his old best friend, Alan Rossini.

In the courtroom, Rossini gave his evidence from behind a high screen that had been placed there to shield him from the public gallery. His every move was flanked by six plainclothes detectives and uniformed officers with shotguns, and dogs checked the building for bombs, and uniformed officers guarded the entrances.

Rossini told the court that it was he who started the chain of events that led to the killing of Michael Hurle and Adam Wright and the wounding of Ronald Singleton outside the Five Dock Hotel on the night of 17 July 1998.

The court heard that Mr Hurle and Mr Singleton were arguing inside the Five Dock Hotel. They had stepped outside to continue their argument and had been joined by Adam Wright when a red station wagon with Shadi Derbas at the wheel stopped at the traffic lights. Rossini yelled out the passenger window: 'Come on, fellas, punch on!'

Mr Singleton and Mr Hurle stopped the fight, yelled 'Bloody wogs' at the car and ran towards it. Mr Singleton grabbed Rossini and pulled him from the car, and four or five of the occupants piled out and started fighting with Mr Wright and Mr Hurle.

'Then I heard gunshots,' said Rossini. He said he saw Michael Kanaan firing shots at close range at their antagonists, hitting Mr Hurle, Mr Wright and Mr Singleton once each with a .22 calibre bullet.

Hit in the stomach, Mr Wright staggered back to the hotel, where he collapsed and died. Mr Singleton was badly wounded in the shoulder. Mr Hurle, who was shot in the chest, fell to the road and grabbed Rossini's trousers as Rossini was trying to get back in the car.

Rossini told the court that Kanaan, who was by now in the back seat of the car, reached out of the window with the revolver and held it point blank at Hurle's head. 'He pulled the trigger a couple of times,' Rossini told the court, 'but nothing happened. I kicked my leg loose and Shadi's taken off.'

Michael Hurle's good fortune didn't last. He died on the way to the hospital.

Rossini alleged that as they drove away, Kanaan said: 'Fuck the Aussies — as long as we're all right we'll do the same thing again.'

The court heard evidence from Michael Kanaan's brother that the accused had been at home playing cards with him and two other men and talking about 'old times' until 11.30 pm on the night in question.

But Rossini's evidence, along with that of another gang member who was there that night and had also turned informer, and the fact that Rossini's and Kanaan's mobile phones had been found at the murder scene, was damning.

It took the jury less than a day to come to a decision, and on 8 August 2001 Michael Kanaan was found guilty of the murders of Adam Wright, Michael Hurle and of the malicious wounding of Ronald Singleton.

On 31 October 2001, after sentencing Michael Kanaan to two terms of life imprisonment without the possibility of parole and to 25 years for malicious wounding, Justice James addressed the court. 'I find each killing was inflicted with intent to kill deliberately and in each case carried out with appalling ruthlessness,' he said. 'What the offender did at the time was a considered, ruthless and vicious series of killings coupled with the wounding. The actions were callous in the extreme.'

But there was still the murder of Danny Karam to be dealt with. And with Alan Rossini, the state's star stool pigeon, still chirping his head off, the result was never going to be a good one for the three men charged: Kanaan, Rabeeh Mawas and Wassim El-Assaad. The fourth conspirator, Charlie Gea Gea, had fled the country in 1999.

At their trial in the Sydney Supreme Court, before Justice James Wood, in May 2002, Rossini told the court that Michael Kanaan was upset that even though it was his and Rossini's efforts that earned the gang an average of around $14,000 a week, Danny Karam held onto most of the profits.

Kanaan was also, he claimed, very upset about Karam's refusal to pay out the $10,000 loan that Kanaan had taken from Kanaan's parents to set up a computer shop as a front to launder drug money.

On top of all that was the successful drug-growing project that Kanaan and Rossini had started only to be ripped off by their boss. Funded by Karam, they had leased a house in Parramatta, in Sydney's western suburbs, and hydroponically cultivated a crop of highly potent marijuana.

After six months, their first crop — 7 kg — was ready for sale. They showed it to Karam, who promptly sold the lot for around $60,000 and kept all the proceeds. The second batch of 3.5 kg was also shown to Karam, who sold it for $30,000. Rossini told the court that Karam not only pocketed all the money from the second sale, but also flew into an uncontrollable rage when his minions couldn't produce a receipt for a $50 piece of hydroponic equipment they had purchased to grow the plants.

Rossini told the court that Kanaan's resentment built daily. He was alleged to have said on numerous occasions: 'After all the work we've done for Danny, to build up this business, we've got nothing for it.'

With the support of all of DK's Boys — because of a promise that they would all be looked after when Danny was dead and Kanaan and Rossini were running the outfit — Kanaan and Rossini set about plotting his murder.

Their first attempt to kill Karam was with a 'hot shot' — a dose of heroin containing a contaminate — but it failed when he became suspicious of the heroin purchased for him by his trusted aide, Charlie Gea Gea. Given that Karam had been shooting up on nothing but pure heroin for years, he was considered a connoisseur of the narcotic, and it was always going to be a tough assignment to get him to inject himself with smack that looked remotely suspicious. Not liking the look of what his lackey had acquired on his behalf, the boss had rejected it, and in doing so had saved his own life, albeit temporarily.

It was decided that the next time the boss visited their safe house, five of the Boys would execute him after he had returned to his car. Anticipating where Karam would park, they had a few practice runs, working out how to avoid killing each other with crossfire, before their plan was ready to be put into action.

On the night that had been scheduled for the execution, 13 December 1998, Danny Karam turned up at the safe house unannounced. He usually rang ahead to let his Boys know he was on his way, but this time he was pressing on the buzzer without any notice at 8.30 pm, a lot earlier than usual.

As El-Assaad buzzed Karam into the building, the elected shooters — Kanaan, Mawas and Gea Gea — hastily grabbed their handguns and jackets, raced out the door, down the stairs, through the underground garage which led out onto the street, and set up their positions around Karam's new aqua Toyota RAV 4, which was parked on the corner of Riley and Fitzroy Streets.

Inside the apartment Karam was greeted by Rossini and El-Assaad and had a cup of coffee and smoked a cone of pot before leaving at just before 9 pm. El-Assaad rang Kanaan on the mobile to tell him that their target was on the way down.

As soon as the unsuspecting drug boss settled in behind the driver's seat, Kanaan, Mawas and Gea Gea opened fire, striking their target 16 times in the head and chest. After the initial onslaught, Kanaan went up to his old boss and shot him once more in the head, for good measure.

Rossini told the court that Kanaan told him after the shooting: 'When Danny was in the car, he saw me and smiled at me. I pulled out the gun, smiled, nodded my head and went [motioning as if to fire a handgun].'

Rossini also alleged that Mawas told him: 'Fuck, I shot him a lot.'

For the defence, Ngaarie Zahabe said that she was sitting in her car in Riley Street, Surry Hills, when she saw three men approach Karam's car. Two of them shot him repeatedly at close range. 'I'm not certain of the amount of times they fired,' Mrs Zahabe told the court. 'But it must have been at least 15 or 16 times — until their guns were empty, I suppose.'

Mrs Zahabe said she saw the three men, of 'Islander appearance', standing in a well-lit area outside the block of flats just before the shooting. When asked if she thought either Kanaan or Mawas was involved in the shooting she replied, 'No.'

The jury deliberated for four and a half days, and on 6 June 2002 they returned a guilty verdict for all three accused. On 29 August 2002, 27-year-old Michael Kanaan was sentenced to another term of life imprisonment without the possibility of parole — on top of the two life sentences he was already serving for the Five Dock murders.

Mawas was given 25 years with a non-parole period of 19 years and El-Assaad received 24 years with a non-parole period of 18 years.

In May 2003 Charbel 'Charlie' Gea Gea, who had fled Australia in 1999, was found guilty and convicted by a Beirut court of the murder of Danny Karam in Surry Hills in December 1998, and sentenced to 20 years in a Lebanon prison.

Australia does not have an extradition treaty with Lebanon, but under Lebanese law a citizen can be tried for crimes committed in another country. Gea Gea is a dual Australian and Lebanese citizen. He is the last man to be arrested and convicted in relation to the Karam killing.

Gea Gea's lawyers indicated that they will appeal the 20-year sentence. Gea Gea is expected to serve his time in the overcrowded Roumieh Jail outside Beirut, where authorities recently launched an inquiry into inmates' claims of daily torture and beatings.

Michael Kanaan, the killer with a heart of stone, is regarded within the prison system as an 'extremely high risk' to other prisoners and the guards. He is under surveillance 24 hours a day in the 'Super Max' — the impenetrable fortress reserved only for the worst of the worst — of Goulburn jail, in southern New South Wales.

It is here that he will most likely spend the rest of his life.

Chapter 7

THE COP KILLER

Bandali Michael Debs

Just after midnight on 16 August 1998, Sergeant Gary
Silk and Senior Constable (SC) Rodney Miller were
shot and killed as they took part in an undercover
police stake-out. Sergeant Silk was killed as he lay
wounded on the ground, and SC Miller died later in
hospital from gunshot wounds. Their killers fled the
scene and escaped. It would be almost two years before
they were captured.

The events leading up to the murders of Sergeant
Silk and SC Miller began in early March 1998, with a
series of armed robberies of what the police termed
'soft targets' — small businesses and restaurants in
Melbourne's southeastern suburbs whose proprietors
would not expect to be held up and therefore would
offer little or no resistance.

The robbers were two men: one a tall, solidly built
older man with receding grey hair who was obviously
the boss, the other a shorter, skinny, dark-haired young
man, seemingly just out of his teens. They could easily
have been a father and son.

Wearing rubber face masks or stockings and
carrying guns, they made a violent and deadly team as
they burst in through the front doors of the

establishments they had selected. They bound and gagged their targets and their targets' clientele with insulation tape, then held guns to their heads and threatened to blow their brains out if they didn't co-operate in handing over the takings and/or their purses, wallets and jewellery. Some of these people were left severely traumatised.

They racked up a string of identical robberies before they murdered Gary Silk and Rodney Miller. The first was a hold-up of Bevic Auto in Carrum Downs. This happened at 5.50 pm — at the end of the day's trading.

Three weeks later they hit the Sportsmart store in nearby Noble Park at 5 pm, just as it was about to close up. Yelling threats and waving handguns around, the robbers told the store's customers and staff that they were prepared to kill everyone and that they wouldn't care if the death toll exceeded that of a recent US high-school massacre.

As in their previous robbery, the bandits bound everyone in the store, including a mother and her 3-year-old child. The store manager later told police that if the robbery hadn't been so horrific she would have burst out laughing, because the younger bandit's face — he was the one who was doing most of the yelling and threatening — was clearly visible through the stocking he had on as a mask. She said she would have had no problem whatever identifying him in a line-up.

At around midnight on 19 April 1998, the bandits burst into the Treasure Chinese Restaurant in Springvale Road, Forest Hill. They confronted the manager and two staff as they were having their supper after closing the restaurant. The manager told police that the two men, who were carrying handguns and wearing masks and 'looking like bears', ordered them all to lie on the floor and told him to hand over the $4000 takings, which he did.

He said that the younger of the two taped their mouths while the older, calmer man remained by the door, calling out orders. The manager said that the one taping them up appeared to be unfamiliar with what he was doing; he asked the older man whether he should tie them up 'hands and feet as well'.

After collecting the takings, plus a watch and a mobile phone, the older man ordered his young partner to grab him a beer out of the fridge and the two took off.

While initially these robberies weren't serious enough to warrant being allocated to the major armed robbery squad, they were soon brought to that squad's attention because they had a very familiar ring to them. Between 1991 and 1994, an older man and a young accomplice had carried out 28 armed robberies of a remarkably similar nature — and they too had targeted small businesses, restaurants and corner stores across the suburbs of Melbourne.

They had appeared at their targets' front doors in masks, around or after closing time, waving guns and demanding money and valuables before tying up their victims. So frequent were these hold-ups that police had formed Task Force Pigout to catch the robbers.

After hold-up number 28 — when the two men narrowly escaped being caught — the bandits' stolen car was found burned out and they disappeared. Their activities came to an abrupt halt. Until, apparently, now. With this history in mind the armed robbery squad took over the investigation.

The robbers seemed to be committing their crimes with total lack of fear of capture. Their sixth victim in this new spree was the Jumbo Chinese Restaurant in Blackburn on the night of 8 June 1998, and they again tied up the owners and patrons and escaped with cash and jewellery — and bottles of expensive alcohol from behind the bar.

On 28 June the robbers struck at the Jade Chinese Restaurant in Kew, just after closing time. The manager told police that there were about 10 staff sitting down to dinner when two men wearing masks — this time of politicians' faces — forced their way in and told everyone to lie on the ground. The robbers then emptied the till and took the more expensive bottles of spirits from behind the bar.

After the bandits' tenth hold-up, during which customers and staff at the Green Papaya Restaurant in Surrey Hills were savagely provoked at gunpoint and told to pass on ominous warnings to police, the armed robbery squad set up an operation — codenamed Hamada — to catch these men.

Out of the about 70 restaurants in the area where the hold-ups had been taking place, Operation Hamada officers decided to stake out the 10 that they believed were the most likely to be the next targets. One of those restaurants was the upmarket Silky Emperor Restaurant, in an industrial estate in Moorabbin.

On the night of Friday, 14 August 1998, the 60 participating officers began their undercover operation. They went to their designated spots and waited. The officers staking out the Silky Emperor Restaurant were Sergeant Gary Silk, 35, from St Kilda station, and Senior Constable Rod Miller, 34, who was based at

Prahran. Both were career policemen and popular with their workmates. Sergeant Silk was single, and his career was his life. SC Miller was married with a 7-week-old son, and hoped to become a detective.

That first night, nothing happened. The following night Silk and Miller, who were in civilian clothes, sat in their unmarked green Holden Commodore down the street from a Korean restaurant in East Bentleigh until it closed at around 10.30 pm. Again, nothing happened.

Concerned that one unit may not be enough to cover the grounds around the Silky Emperor Restaurant, which closed later, their superior, Detective Sergeant (DS) Butterworth, moved them to an underground car park close to the restaurant to back up two other officers, Senior Detective (SD) Darren Sherren and SC Frank Bendeich, who were already parked in a nearby hardware store car park. They didn't have to wait long for a possible suspect.

Jeffrey Dean, a criminal with an extensive record for breaking and entering and stealing from cars, had been cruising the area in his car. He had already broken into a couple of cars earlier that evening and stolen money and credit cards. Dean thought that the car park of the busy Silky Emperor Restaurant would be easy pickings. Until he recognised the plates of the Commodore with two men sitting in it as those used on unmarked Victorian police vehicles, that is.

Dean immediately saw that the police officers were watching him. Realising that he and his car looked out of place and would be in trouble if the police decided to pull him over and have a chat with him, he slowly did a U-turn, then planted his foot and accelerated up the exit ramp, jumped a gutter and disappeared in a cloud of smoke.

Silk and Miller started up their car and gave chase, but Dean was gone. The two policemen drove back to their designated spot in the car park, stopping to talk briefly with officers Sherren and Bendeich on the way.

Just after midnight, Silk and Miller observed a dark blue Hyundai Excel enter the car park, drive around and then drive off. In the policemen's judgment the driver of the vehicle was acting suspiciously enough to warrant being pulled over, so, with a blue light flashing on the roof, the officers took off after the Hyundai. It appeared to have just one occupant. Officers Sherren and Bendeich saw what was happening from their spot in the hardware store car park; they started their vehicle and followed the pursuit, staying about 100 metres back.

The Hyundai driver didn't appear to be in any hurry. Obviously aware that there was a police car with lights flashing not far behind, the driver pulled over outside a panel-beating shop around the corner, in Cochranes Road. The police car pulled up behind it. Both Silk and Miller got out and approached the Hyundai. A man stepped out and into the headlights of the police car.

As Sergeant Silk began to question the man, the back-up vehicle containing officers Sherren and Bendeich cruised slowly past, U-turned and sat about 100 metres away, watching proceedings.

Silk noticed another man — considerably younger than the man he was questioning — hiding in the car. Silk told Miller to keep an eye on the first man, and called to the second man to get out of the car. He instructed the man to walk away from the vehicle and out of earshot, so that the two men couldn't work together on their stories.

As Silk was about to start taking notes, the younger man produced a .38 revolver and shot him once in the chest at point blank range. As the officer slumped to the ground the man aimed at him again and fired, but the gun misfired and the bullet fell harmlessly to the ground.

SC Miller drew out his service revolver and fired twice at the man who had shot his partner, but missed both times. The bullets lodged in the roller shutter door of the panel-beating shop.

Now unguarded, the older man reached into the Hyundai and produced a .357 Magnum, took aim at Miller, who was now standing just behind the Hyundai, and fired — but missed. The bullet shattered the Hyundai's rear window, spraying glass fragments all over the road.

Miller ran to take cover behind the police car. He dropped to his knees, and with his head pressed against the tail light, returned fire with his .38 Smith and Wesson. He didn't score a hit. The older man shot back, and Miller was hit — a bullet entered his upper chest and exited through his right hip.

Under fire and gravely wounded, Miller staggered in the direction of the Silky Emperor Restaurant, returning fire as he went, and disappeared around a service station on the corner.

Turning his attention to Silk, who lay unconscious on the nature strip, the older man fired a bullet into the stricken officer's hip and then made sure of the job with another shot at point blank range behind the officer's left ear. Gary Silk never had a chance to defend himself.

This all happened so quickly — the shootout lasted just seconds, during which at least 11 shots were fired — that it wasn't until Sergeant Silk was dead and SC Miller had staggered away from scene that the two officers in the back-up car, Sherren and Bendeich, realised what was going on.

SD Sherren yelled a 'shots fired, shots fired' warning into the police two-way radio in their car, then he and Bendeich headed to the boot for their bulletproof vests. The Hyundai headed straight at them, but swerved to miss them at the last second and sped off.

Most concerned now for the safety of their fellow officers, Sherren and Bendeich raced to where the shots had come from. They found Silk lying on his side on the nature strip, which was soaked in blood from a gaping bullet hole in his head. He had no pulse.

Guns and torches in hand, Sherren and Bendeich cautiously searched the immediate area for Miller. Meanwhile, almost 200 metres away, at the Silky Emperor Restaurant, staff had called 000 after they had mistakenly identified SC Miller as a drunk waving a gun on the footpath outside the restaurant.

The manager later told police that he and his staff had been terrified as the man writhed in agony and pleaded for help on the steps of the restaurant; he had tried to get up, only to fall back over, and had been calling out, 'Help, help!'

The manager and staff had no way of knowing who he was — he was in ordinary clothes, and there was nothing to indicate that he was a police officer. They had assumed that he had been involved in some criminal activity, so they had dialled 000. By the time they did this, there were police officers from every direction speeding towards the crime scene in response to Sherren's call for help.

SC Miller was found by officers Sherren and Bendeich lying on the footpath outside the restaurant. He had been shot once in the chest and stomach but was still alive and conscious. Although badly wounded and in pain, SC Miller was able to give the officers a brief description of the two men, what they were wearing, and the colour, make and model of their car.

Within minutes SC Miller was in an ambulance and on his way to hospital. However, he suffered cardiac arrest on the trip and lapsed into a coma. He died — without ever regaining consciousness — during emergency surgery at the Monash Medical Centre.

Despite Miller's description of the killers and their car, investigators had little to go on. All they got from the crime scene were the fragments of glass from the killers' car, the bullets that had stayed in the roller shutter door at the front of the panel beater's shop and the bullet that had fallen from the misfired gun — though at the time, they had no way of knowing why that bullet happened to be where it was.

Investigators assumed that the killers' car must have had local plates — if it had had interstate plates, SC Miller would have told them. The only other possible witness was a drunken driver who had pulled over into a nearby car park to sleep it off. He said that he heard the commotion but went back to sleep; he could offer no useful information.

Within days Task Force Lorimer — the biggest in Victoria's history — was set up to catch the cop killers.

The 35 experienced detectives assigned to investigate their comrades' murders were told by their leader, Detective Inspector (DI) Ian Sheridan, that though it was likely to be a long and relentless investigation, no matter what, in the long run they would get their men.

In response to a police request for help from the public, the Crime Stoppers phone line had 5500 calls in 10 days, and police switchboards recorded 2500 information calls within two weeks. Each call had to be followed up.

Operation Hamada suspects who had previously been under suspicion for the armed hold-ups were called on and asked for an alibi for the night of the murders. All were accounted for.

The best lead the police had was the dark blue Hyundai Excel, of which there were approximately 200,000 in Australia. A team of 250 officers across Victoria painstakingly went about eliminating as many of these as they could, in the hope that eventually they would be left with only a few hundred that warranted further investigation.

Other members of the task force, led by DS Mick Ritchie, notified every spare parts dealer and wrecking yard that if anyone inquired about a rear window for that model, the dealer was to notify the team immediately. They checked out stolen car records, rental cars, unregistered Excels and write-offs.

On 28 August, in response to a call from Grant Walker Spare Parts saying that they had just sold a Hyundai rear windscreen to two people who said that someone had smashed the glass in an attempt to steal the car's stereo, DS Ritchie and Senior Detective (SD) Simon Illingworth arrived at the home of the car's owner, Nicole Debs, and spoke with her and her boyfriend, Jason Roberts.

Nicole Debs told the officers that her father, a tiler, had borrowed the car, and had broken the windscreen three days after the murder, when he was carting some brass tiling strips to a job in Hallam. Ms Debs said her father, Bandali Debs, wasn't there at the moment, but she would arrange a time for police to come back and interview him.

Three days later the officers returned and spoke to Bandali Debs, who repeated his daughter's story and said that he could provide his mobile phone records to support it. As there was nothing to indicate that Debs had been involved in the murders and there was nothing to refute his story, the officers put him down as another lead that had been followed up but had come to nothing. Just the same, they left the book open on Bandali Debs and his daughter.

To narrow down the search for the Hyundai, in December 1998 forensic officers from Task Force Lorimer went to the Hyundai plant in South Korea, in the hope that they might turn up something that could save them lots of leg work. They did.

Engineers at the factory told them that the glass fragments from the murder vehicle's rear windscreen only came from the X3 model three-door or five-door hatchbacks which were built in March 1997. This narrowed the field of eligible Hyundais down to just over 2600 of the 35,000 vehicles in Victoria. The number of man-hours saved by this one discovery was incalculable.

In the meantime, detectives had physically checked out more than 1250 positive leads and interviewed more than 400 potential suspects: these included paroled killers, drug dealers, bank robbers, car thieves and their associates. But if any of them knew anything about the killings they weren't talking. By the time the investigation was over, police would have interviewed over 3000 possible suspects.

One of the 2600 eligible Hyundais was that of Nicole Debs. Task force detectives went to see her again. This time — in order to eliminate the car rather than because they were suspicious — the police took the car away for further examination at the Victorian Police Forensic Science Centre.

Further examination of the vehicle found nothing to indicate that it was the suspect vehicle. Tests on fragments of glass found in the car proved inconclusive.

The following day the car was returned to Nicole Debs and a week later, as a matter of routine, detectives returned. They took further statements from Nicole and her father, and from Nicole's boyfriend, Jason Roberts, and after final checks were made, they were all cleared of suspicion.

The investigation was now into its fifth month, and was at a dead end. DI Ian Sheridan ordered his task force to go back through every piece of evidence and interview in the hope that they had missed something. He was right: they had.

When the phone number of a criminal who was deemed a person of interest in the inquiry was cross-checked on the police computer with all the other people who had been questioned, it showed that there had been a lot of phone traffic between this individual and Bandali Debs — indicating to the investigators that beneath his apparently clean-skin exterior, the allegedly hardworking tiler had some involvement with at least one criminal.

DI Sheridan instructed his forensics team to take a longer and harder look at the fragments of glass taken from Nicole Debs' car. They were a perfect match with the fragments found at the murder scene.

The photo on Jason Roberts' driver's licence was compared with the identikit of one of the bandits in the Sportsmart robbery. The likeness was striking. When shown the photo, the witness who had compiled the identikit identified Roberts immediately as one of the men who had robbed the shop. This was the woman who had said his face was clearly visible through the stocking he had on as a mask.

Quietly confident that they had their killers, in October 1999, in absolute secrecy, police were given permission to tap Bandali and Nicole Debs' and Jason Roberts' mobile phones, and to place concealed listening devices in their cars and homes. All three were now under around-the-clock surveillance.

By early 2000, all the eligible Hyundai Excels in Victoria — hatchbacks manufactured in March 1997 — had been accounted for, and by the time police had tracked down the remaining 1000 or so around the country, there was only one Excel fitted with that particular windscreen that could have been the murder vehicle. Its registration was OJI–862 and it belonged to Nicole Debs.

The audio surveillance revealed that Bandali Debs had no idea that the police were on to him. The tapes disclosed some terrifying information. In February 2000, Debs told a daughter that he had toyed with the idea of killing two more police officers on the other side of Melbourne, to 'make the investigation spread stupidly', and that he had also contemplated killing SC Miller's widow and infant son.

In July 2000, DI Sheridan played a trump card. Asking the public if they knew this man, he released to the press a computerised image of the photo on Roberts' driver's licence. He wanted to see if it would intimidate Roberts. It did.

The following morning Jason Roberts presented himself to the Cranbourne police station and asked if the picture was meant to be him. Roberts was asked to come back in three days; when he did, he was interviewed by task force detectives for three hours.

Several days later, on 25 July 2000, task force detectives arrested Bandali Debs and Roberts and raided Debs' mother's house in Sydney, where they found buried jewellery and guns. Debs was charged with the murders of the two police officers. Roberts was released under tight surveillance in the hope that he would unwittingly provide police with further incriminating evidence.

Jason Roberts went straight to the newspapers, protesting his innocence. It didn't do him any good. On 15 August, just one day short of the second anniversary of the killings, he was arrested and charged with the murders of Sergeant Gary Silk and Senior Constable Rodney Miller.

When they interviewed Debs' friends and workmates, police found out that the windscreen on the Hyundai had been broken around the same time that the two policemen were killed — earlier than Debs and Roberts had said. Police pulled the Hyundai apart a bolt at a time. This time they discovered minuscule particles of gunshot propellant where the rear windscreen had been shattered.

By the time Bandali Debs and Jason Roberts went to trial, in September 2002 at the Victorian Supreme Court, presided over by Justice Philip Cummings, the Crown believed it had a watertight case against them.

The court heard that on the night of 15 November 1998, Debs and Roberts were waiting for the Silky Emperor Restaurant to close. When it did, they were going to enter the premises, hold up the proprietor with pistols and steal the evening's takings.

However, Debs and Roberts' plan was foiled by Sergeant Silk and SC Miller, and when the two thieves' car was pulled over by the policemen, they murdered them both in cold blood. The jury heard that the getaway car had been indisputably linked to the accused, and that incriminating conversations between Debs and members of his family had been recorded.

Conversations such as this one, where Debs is talking to his daughter Joanne:

Debs: Look, listen, Joanne. I don't want you to worry or anything but I'm telling you straight. Within the next six months, we're going to have to have to get rid of another two CPs [policemen]. Listen.

Joanne: You need some luck.

Debs: No, no. Ya know why? To make the investigation just spread stupidly.

Joanne: Yeah but what for? They've already been here.

Debs: Ah.

Joanne: Right. They've questioned, taken the car. If they found anything on that car, don't you think that they would have been fuckin' pullin' yous both into the police station by now?'

Debs in a later conversation with his daughter Joanne:

Debs: But I'm telling you now. If this continues like this, on this matter, two CPs have got to go down somewhere, so the investigation goes stupid.

Joanne: Yeah. But where? It's got to be far, though.

Debs: It's got to be out of the area.

Joanne: Hmm.

Debs: It could be . . .

Joanne: Across the other side of the city.

Debs: On the other side of the city.

Joanne: That's where it's gotta be, though.

Debs: Yeah.

Joanne: It has to be.

Debs: Yeah. So it fucks the whole situation up. And we can't go through e-tag [which automatically records when you pay your toll] or anything like that.

Joanne: Yeah but you . . .

Debs: Back roads and that's it. I'm tellin' ya.

Debs in a conversation with his elderly father, Malik:

Debs: Those were the ones that were sittin' there, when we drove in just to quickly look. They seen us so they drove behind us and drove down the street to stop us. They stopped us. Then it's not good.

Malik: It's not good?

Debs: Yeah.

Malik: Before then, when everything finished.

Debs: I mean, everything was finished. Nobody was anywhere. Nobody seen anything.

Malik: But when you went, did you see anyone?

Debs: No. Nobody's seen nothin'. Nobody was anywhere.

Malik: Are you sure? Sometimes people do something ...

Debs: A few shots, it's no worries, a little thing.

Malik: That's when they search, hear something ...

Debs: As soon as that happened we went. But then they came, after everything happened they came in one minute.

In another conversation with his father, Debs said: 'All's I done was I squeezed the [inaudible] and then I just went like that [inaudible] ... He was on the ground, lying on the ground, firing in the air.'

Members of the murdered policemen's families wept openly as the court heard this conversation between Debs and Roberts about SC Miller's family:

Debs: Oh no. Ya know the other cunt. The other cunt's father died too. [Gary Silk's father had died of cancer soon after his son had been murdered.]

Roberts: Oh yeah. I know that, but no, this, this Miller, he's about 70. He was, he served in World War I and all this shit ...

Debs: Ah, this, what's his name, ah, Miller was basically orphaned off. He lost every cunt.

Roberts: Did he?

Debs: Yeah.

Roberts: Only his wife. Yeah.

Debs: He, he had only his missus and a fuckin', some fuckin' cockhead kid. Whatever.

Roberts: Ya jokin'. That's all he ... kid. Yeah, he did, didn't he?

Prosecutor Jeremy Rapke, QC, said that it was apparent to him that Debs and Roberts hated police 'with a depth and passion which was almost unimaginable'.

Debs' three daughters — Nicole, 23, Joanne, 22, and Kylie, 21 — sat through most of the trial with Roberts' mother, Marina. Debs' two sons, Michael, 19, and Joseph, 18, joined them for the defence's closing address.

In his client's defence, Ian Hill, QC, acting for Roberts, denied that his client was anywhere near the area at the time of the murders. Mr Hill and Chris Dane, QC, acting for Debs, offered different theories as to what took place just after midnight on 16 August 1998.

Mr Hill told the jury that the officers were shot by a 'lone gunman' who first fired upon Sergeant Silk and then grabbed another gun from the car and killed SC Miller with it.

Mr Hill said that just before he died, SC Miller described his killer as being 'six foot tall', which meant that it could not have been Roberts, who was considerably shorter than that, and suggested that the dying policeman's vision of two offenders must have been distorted.

In total contradiction to Mr Hill's hypothesis, Mr Dane told the jury that his client, Bandali Debs, was at the scene of the crimes on that night but was not guilty of murder because he had not agreed to Roberts shooting Sergeant Silk, and had fired upon SC Miller only in self-defence. Mr Dane also maintained that even if his client did shoot Seargeant Silk in the hip and head after Roberts had shot him, it would not be murder, as he was shooting a man who was already dead. (This theory was not supported by the medical evidence.)

Bandali Michael Debs

On Wednesday, 1 January 2003, after a four-month trial and a five-and-a-half day deliberation by the jury, Bandali Michael Debs, 49, and Jason Joseph Roberts, 22, were found guilty of the murders of Sergeant Gary Silk and Senior Constable Rodney Miller.

On 17 February 2003, Justice Cummings handed down his sentences after hearing final arguments from defence counsel. To Jason Roberts he said, 'I am fully satisfied that you were there and acted murderously there, fully by your own free choice and decision. The only harbinger of rehabilitation in you is your age. Only because of your youth do I consider that a minimum term of imprisonment should be set. I direct you to serve a minimum of 35 years before eligibility for parole.'

In sentencing Bandali Debs, Justice Cummings was not so benevolent:

'Mr Debs, the nature and gravity of your two offences and your past history make the fixing of a minimum term entirely inappropriate. I refuse to set a minimum term.

'Mr Debs, for the murder of Sergeant Silk, I sentence you to life imprisonment. For the murder of Senior Constable Miller, I sentence you to life imprisonment. No minimum term of imprisonment before eligibility for parole is set. You are sentenced to be imprisoned for the remainder of your life.

'Life means life.'

As a result of inquiries made during the Silk/Miller murder investigation, on 18 November 2003 Jason Manuel Ghiller, 27, was sentenced to 10 years in jail with a non-parole period of 6 years.

Ghiller had pleaded guilty to accompanying his uncle, Bandali Debs, in 13 armed robberies of restaurants and takeaway outlets in Melbourne's south between 1991 and 1994. During the robberies Ghiller had also aided and abetted Debs in the shooting of a newsagency owner which left the man paralysed.

Also on 18 November 2003, the Office of Public Prosecutions decided that two of Bandali Debs' daughters, Joanne and Nicole, would not be prosecuted, even though detectives were convinced that they had impeded the investigation.

Chapter 8

THE ORDINARY MONSTER

Peter Norris Dupas

Peter Dupas was a predatory sex monster of the worst kind imaginable. A cruel and calculating man who meticulously went about his depravity and could then melt into a crowd in a heartbeat. A man so ordinary and inconspicuous that it was almost impossible to believe that he could commit such atrocities. And that is the way his victims saw him — and why they allowed him into their company. Time and time again he was allowed back into the community, and time and time again he re-offended.

He left those who survived so traumatised that some could never again go to sleep without the light on or walk down their own hallway unaccompanied. And no sooner was Peter Dupas out of jail than he would re-offend, each time doing something worse than he had done previously, until he killed, and at last was locked away where he would never be allowed to hurt anyone again.

Born into a loving home in Sydney on 6 July 1953, Peter Norris Dupas was the youngest of three children. When he was an infant his family moved to Melbourne, and he grew up in the Frankston and Mount Waverley areas. Peter's brother and sister were many years older than him, which meant that he was treated like an only child by parents who were old enough to be his grandparents. He later claimed that he was a spoilt child, and that he had been made to feel inadequate by his over-protective mother and perfectionist father.

Teased by the other kids at school because he was a slow learner and prone to be overweight — his nickname was Pugsley, after the boy in the sitcom *The Addams Family* — Dupas grew up as the class dunce and repeated Year 7. At age 15 Dupas began his criminal career, using the style that would become his trademark — attacking women with a knife. Later he would add a balaclava.

On 3 October 1968 — while wearing his school uniform — Dupas went to the house next door and asked his friendly 27-year-old neighbour, who was nursing her 5-week-old baby, if he could borrow a sharp knife so he could peel some potatoes. As the woman commented on what a good boy he was to be helping his mother with the cooking, he lunged at her with the knife and stabbed her in the stomach without saying a word.

'He knocked me down onto the floor and fell on top of me,' the woman told the police. 'He kept on stabbing me with the knife and I kept trying to ward him off. I felt the knife cut into my hands — mainly my right hand — and my face and my neck.

'I was holding onto the knife at one stage, trying to break the blade. I was lying on my back and he was sitting on top of me. He said; "It's too late, I can't stop now, they'll lock me up."'

After covering her mouth with his hand and repeatedly bashing the woman's head on the floor,

Dupas stopped as abruptly as he had begun. He told police he didn't know why he had attacked his neighbour, and that he would never intentionally hurt anyone.

'I can remember having the knife in my hand,' Dupas told police. 'I must have been trying to kill her or something.'

The teenage assailant was taken to Larundel Hospital for psychiatric assessment. It was concluded in court that he was 'caught in an emotional conflict between the need to conform to the expectations of his parents and the unconscious urges to express his aggression and his developing masculinity'. Dupas was put on 18 months' probation and told to undergo psychiatric treatment.

He left school during what would now be Year 11 but was then the last year of high school, and took up an apprenticeship as a fitter and turner at General Electric, at nearby Notting Hill. While doing his apprenticeship, Dupas applied to join the police force, where he presumably hoped to be able to exert authority legally. He was rejected, though, because he was 1 cm too short.

On 10 March 1972, a man chased and caught 19-year-old Dupas after finding him peeping through the bathroom window while the man's wife was in the shower. On 15 November 1973, Dupas was interviewed by police after a motorist reported that Dupas had repeatedly driven alongside his car, staring and smiling at his 12-year-old daughter.

Two weeks later, detectives from nearby Nunawading arrested and charged Dupas with the rape of a married woman three weeks earlier, on 5

November 1973. They alleged that Dupas had asked his victim for help, claiming his car had broken down outside her home. While the woman was looking for a screwdriver, Dupas hid in the house, then threatened the woman and her 18-month-old baby with a knife before raping her.

Police alleged that in the fortnight before he was picked up Dupas had tricked two other women into letting him into their homes with the same ruse but both times had left without assaulting the women. He stole money from the first house then left, and fled from the second when the woman told him her husband was on the way home and would be there any minute.

Even in those early days, arresting detectives saw the danger in Dupas, and the leader of the investigation, Senior Sergeant Ian Armstrong, described him to reporters as 'an evil, cold, baby-faced liar who would possibly cause the death of one of his victims if he wasn't straightened out'.

The investigating detectives discovered that Dupas was a consummate liar and a very frustrating interview subject — even in the face of overwhelming evidence he would deny everything. Then he would break down, but just when it looked as though he was about to make a confession he would straighten himself up and deny everything again, and they would have to go back and start again from the beginning.

Detectives also discovered that Dupas was not a rapist who attacked only when an opportunity presented itself. There was nothing random about his approach. He would have everything worked out down to the last detail. Once he had chosen his victim, he would go about his business in a very cold and calculated fashion, remaining calm at all times, even when arrested.

'He was a cool, cunning liar,' Detective Armstrong told reporters. 'You'd look at him and think, could he be this callous, this dangerous? But I knew this guy would be a danger … you could smell it.'

After being charged with rape and released on bail, Dupas was remanded to Mont Park psychiatric hospital, from which he was allowed to come and go as he pleased. While still attending Mont Park, Dupas was arrested for a series of incidents on the nearby Rosebud Beach foreshore.

He was seen on at least three occasions entering a female toilet and shower block and watching girls showering, and was then trapped in a police stakeout. He was taken back to Mont Park and admitted as a voluntary patient. He then stayed put for a few weeks — from 8 January 1974 to 22 February.

Charged with loitering with intent and offensive behaviour over the Rosebud incidents, the court heard that while psychiatrists at Mont Park were unable to find any gross psychiatric disorder with the 21-year-old Dupas, they did not exclude the possibility of personality problems for him in the future. Dupas was fined $140.

Six months later, at his sentencing for the Nunawading rape, the judge was not so lenient. County Court Judge John Leckie didn't hold back as he berated Dupas for what he described as one of the most appalling crimes. 'You raped a young married woman who was previously unknown to you in her own home and on her own bed,' he said to the prisoner. 'You invaded the sanctity of her home by a false story about your car breaking down. You threatened her with a knife, you tied her up with a cord, you struck her when she tried to resist and, worst of all, you threatened to harm her baby when she tried to resist.

'Whilst accepting that you are psychologically disturbed,' Judge Leckie said, 'I believe you were fully responsible for your actions.'

And in what would be a fatally accurate prediction, Dr Allen Bartholomew, one of Australia's most experienced forensic psychiatrists who had examined Dupas while he was in custody, told the court, 'I am reasonably certain that this youth has a serious psychosexual problem, and that he is using the technique of denial as a coping device. He is to be seen as potentially dangerous.'

Judge Leckie sentenced Dupas to nine years' jail with a non-parole period of five years.

Jail and attempts at rehabilitation obviously had no effect on Peter Dupas, because just a little more than two months after his release — he was released on 4 September 1979, after serving five years and eight months — he attacked four women over a 10-day period, leaving each one psychologically damaged. This time he was equipped with what would become his trademark — a knife and a balaclava.

Dupas raped his first victim in a Frankston public toilet block. His next three victims escaped, but one, an elderly woman, was stabbed in the chest as she offered as much resistance as she could muster in an attempt to escape. His attempt at rape foiled, Dupas bolted. The woman told police that it wasn't until she started getting to her feet after her assailant had run away and saw blood pouring from the left side of her chest that she realised she had been stabbed.

When Dupas was picked up by police, he confessed to all the attacks. He said he was glad that he had been caught and that he had fled from the last two attempted assaults when the women started screaming. His only explanation for the attacks was that he 'gets the urge'.

Dupas told arresting officers in a record of interview, 'It just comes over me. I can't help myself. I have had this problem for about six years. It all started again about a year ago. I don't know if it was because me [sic] girlfriend left me or what it is. I just find it hard to mix with people and I haven't many friends. I just don't know what to say.'

Dupas was charged with rape, three counts of assault with intent to rape, malicious wounding, indecent assault and assault with intent to rob. Judge Leo Lazarus presided over the case, and when Dupas was found guilty on all counts, the judge shocked the prosecution by handing down what they considered a light sentence: six years with, again, a five-year non-parole period. This was despite the fact that it was Dupas's second time round for rape and that he was being convicted on several more charges than previously.

He was released on 27 February 1985, after serving five years and three months. Four days later, Dupas raped a 21-year-old receptionist as she lay sunbaking at Blairgowrie back beach. Two men the distraught victim had asked for help caught Dupas as he was walking away from the beach — he had misplaced his car.

Dupas could offer no explanation for his behaviour: he said that he had been enjoying himself on the beach, having an easy day 'laying back', when he saw the woman and couldn't help himself. Dupas said that he was sorry for the attack, and that everyone had assured him that he was all right now, and that all he wanted to do was live a normal life.

Dupas also couldn't help police with their inquiries into a murder that had taken place 16 days earlier — while he was on temporary leave from prison. Helen McMahon, a mother of four, had been beaten to death while sunbathing in the sand dunes at Rye back beach, 4 km away.

Once again in court for rape, Dupas was not as fortunate this time as he had been with Judge Leo Lazarus. Instead, he had to front Judge John Leckie, the same judge who had verbally caned him before sentencing him to five years' jail on the Nunawading rape 11 years earlier. To add to Dupas's woes, Judge Leckie had been critical of the sentence handed down by Judge Lazarus, saying it was 'inadequate'.

Judge Leckie told the court that in his opinion, Judge Lazarus's attempt to rehabilitate Dupas five years earlier had 'failed miserably' — he described Dupas as 'walking around with a loaded time bomb in his pocket'.

Judge Leckie sentenced Dupas to 12 years in prison with a 10-year non-parole period.

In prison Dupas underwent medical treatment to reduce his sex drive. In 1987, while still a prisoner in Castlemaine Jail, Dupas married a nurse 16 years his senior, whom he met while she was working in G Division. A Mont Park psychiatrist said later, talking about this time in Dupas's life, 'He believes all of that [his sex attacks] is behind him since he understands himself better and has become more assertive.'

Released on 3 March 1992, after serving exactly seven years, Dupas lay low for 18 months, until on 23 September 1993 he attacked a 15-year-old girl who was horseriding at Kyneton. Fortunately, the girl had the common sense to put her horse between herself and Dupas, and she escaped physically unhurt. Dupas escaped unidentified.

On 3 January 1994, at 11.30 in the morning, Dupas attacked a 26-year-old bank teller who was spending the weekend with her fiancé and three friends at a holiday house near Lake Eppalock in northwestern Victoria. As she sat on the toilet in a public toilet block he burst into the cubicle, wearing a hood with eye holes and pointing a knife at her face.

Dupas kept yelling for the woman to turn around and face the wall but she resisted. She was cut badly on the hands as she fought to prevent her attacker dragging her out of the toilet cubicle. Thwarted, Dupas abruptly stopped the attack, let the woman go and calmly walked away to his car.

As Dupas sped off, the woman identified him to her fiancé, who was an off-duty Australian Federal Police officer. With friends, he chased the station wagon for 15 km and overpowered Dupas after his car ran off into the bush on a dirt road.

Police found a roll of insulation tape and a pair of metal handcuffs in Dupas's pockets. In his car they found a grisly cache: the tools of trade of a well-prepared travelling rapist. He had knives, a black balaclava, condoms, a roll of sticking plaster and — chillingly — a sheet of plastic and a shovel.

Despite what police saw as Dupas's meticulous planning for a sexual abduction, murder and concealment of a body, disappointed prosecutors told Judge Leo Hart that they did not have enough evidence to sustain a charge of attempted rape against Dupas; the charge would have to be reduced to false imprisonment.

It was a bitter blow to police and the prosecution, especially because under recently introduced Victorian legislation designed to deal more severely with serial sex offenders — and Dupas was the perfect example, with his litany of previous convictions — they could have put him away for an indefinite period, possibly forever, so that he couldn't harm any more women.

Dupas pleaded guilty to false imprisonment, and Judge Hart sentenced him to three years and nine months' jail, with a minimum of two years and nine months.

During the proceedings, the court had been told that the woman Dupas attacked and tried to abduct was still too scared to even walk down the passage from her bedroom to the toilet at night.

Dupas served the minimum term and was released on 29 September 1996 to find that his wife had left him. He got a job as a factory hand and lived for a short time in a flat in Rose Street, Brunswick, and later moved in with a woman who knew nothing of his background. She lived in Coanne Street, Pascoe Vale, near the busy shopping area in Cumberland Road.

On 4 October 1997 a local prostitute and recovering heroin addict, 40-year-old Margaret Maher, who shopped at Pascoe Vale regularly, was abducted and murdered. Ms Maher's body was found in long grass on industrial land near Cliffords Road, Somerton. Ms Maher had been stabbed many times and her breasts had been grotesquely mutilated.

Four weeks to the day later, on 1 November 1997, Mersina Halvagis, 25, was repeatedly stabbed and left to die between graves as she was laying flowers on the grave of her grandmother in nearby Fawkner Cemetery. By a strange coincidence, the grave of Peter Dupas's grandfather is also at Fawkner Cemetery, only 100 metres away from where Ms Halvagis was murdered.

At 6.30 am on New Year's Eve 1997, Kathleen Downes, a frail 95-year-old who had suffered two strokes and used a walking frame, was found stabbed to death in her room at Brunswick Lodge nursing home, where she had lived for eight years. Detectives established that phone calls were made from Dupas's Pascoe Vale home to the Brunswick nursing home in the weeks before Mrs Downes's death. They were unable to establish any previous link between the two addresses or any reason for the calls to have been made.

At around six o'clock on the evening of 19 April 1999, Rena Hoffman called around to her friend Nicole Patterson's Westgarth home for tea. Ms Hoffman became concerned when she couldn't get a response, so she entered the house — where Ms Patterson worked from home as a psychotherapist — and found her friend dead on her consulting room floor.

Ms Patterson was naked from the waist down. Her clothes had been ripped and cut. 'I saw Nicky arranged, naked, and there was blood near her, not actually on her,' Ms Hoffman told police. 'She seemed cleaned up or something.'

An autopsy revealed that 28-year-old Nicole Patterson had been dead since that morning. She had been stabbed 27 times. There were numerous defensive wounds to both her hands. It was impossible to say whether or not she had been raped. Both Ms Patterson's breasts had been sliced off — they were nowhere to be found at the murder scene. The mutilation of Ms Patterson was the same as that of Margaret Maher, who had been murdered on 4 October 1997.

A neighbour of Ms Patterson had heard a woman scream at 9.30 am, and another witness had heard two shouts around the same time. Another neighbour said he heard 'a scream of pain, not fear', and about 10 minutes later saw a man walking with 'a sort of intentness' from the direction of Ms Patterson's house.

The killer had been thorough. He had cleaned up after himself. There were no finger- or footprints. It looked as if the house had been wiped down, and as if the killer had scoured the premises to make sure he had not left any clues. He had even taken Ms Patterson's purse, containing her driver's licence and her mobile phone.

But the killer had missed the most incriminating piece of evidence. Under clothing on the lounge, detectives found Ms Patterson's appointment book. It had a 9 am appointment for a 'Malcolm' listed for that morning, with a mobile phone number written next to the name.

'Malcolm' turned out to be a student who had no idea who Ms Patterson was. 'Had he given out his phone number to anyone recently?' the police asked. He had, and he gave police a list. One of the names he was doing a bit of handy work for, Peter Dupas, came up like a rash on the computer.

Police put what they had together. Ms Patterson advertised her business in the local papers, so it wouldn't be hard to arrange to get into her house. Her killer had made an appointment under a false name for that morning, using a false mobile phone number. What he didn't count on was police finding the appointment book.

When police raided Dupas's home — which was less than 30 minutes' drive from where Ms Patterson was murdered — three days after the murder, Dupas had a fingernail scratch on his face. A search of the premises uncovered a bloodstained green jacket in a bundle of clothing in a workshop cupboard. DNA testing showed that there was less than a 1 in 6.5 billion chance that the blood in 13 of the 14 drops on the jacket did not belong to Ms Patterson. The other drop was Dupas's blood mixed with Ms Patterson's.

Investigators also found a black balaclava and a page from the *Herald Sun* with a report of the murder on it. The photo of Nicole Patterson in the article had been slashed. In Dupas's garbage bin police found torn-up pieces of newspaper; when the pieces were put together they formed a handwritten note with the words 'nine o'clock Nicci' and 'Malcolm' written on it. Police also confirmed that on the day of the killing, Dupas was caught on video buying petrol near Ms Patterson's home.

Despite the mountain of circumstantial evidence, Dupas denied any knowledge of Ms Patterson's death, saying only that the police must have planted the evidence on him in order to get a conviction. Peter Dupas was charged with the murder of Nicole Patterson, and was remanded in custody until the trial.

To her family and friends and anyone who had even been remotely in touch with her throughout her life, Nicole Patterson's death was cruel and pointless. A horrible waste of a thoroughly decent person. Nicole didn't have an enemy in the world. Of all of the things that an attractive, athletic and intelligent young woman could have done with her life, she chose psychotherapy, and dedicated much of her time to helping young people with drug problems.

In her spare time, Nicole worked as a youth counsellor at the Ardoch Centre, an organisation which endeavours to assist homeless or disadvantaged young people. She also participated in activities associated with the Australia Drug Foundation.

Nicole's life was focused on three things: her work, her partner of 20 months, Richard Smith, and her beloved dog, Bella, whom she had rescued from an animal shelter. Her sister Kylie said of Nicole, 'She was the most beautiful person I've known, and she had a lot of special gifts that not many people have.'

Early in 1999, Nicole had set up the front bedroom of her home as a consulting room, and then started advertising for clients in the local papers.

Putting the pieces together, investigators believed that the man calling himself 'Malcolm' made the first of 15 phone calls to her on 3 March and eventually made an appointment for 9 am on 19 April, on the pretext that he wanted to consult her about his chronic gambling problem.

Police believed that Dupas arrived at 9 am and was ushered into the consulting room, and that he then attacked Nicole as she was making coffee for them both. Dupas set upon her, they said, stabbing her viciously and repeatedly with a knife he had brought with him. Nicole put up strong resistance, as was indicated by the shouting heard by the neighbours and the cuts to her hands.

Once he had murdered Nicole, the prosecution claimed, Dupas set about fastidiously cleaning up the room and removing any clues that could lead to him. Then he took his souvenirs — Nicole's purse and her body parts. But fortunately for investigators, he missed the diary that led them straight to his door.

At his trial, held at the Supreme Court of Victoria before Justice Frank Vincent in August 2000, Dupas, who described his occupation as a part-time furniture maker, told the court that all the evidence must have been planted by police because he had never been to Nicole Patterson's Westgarth home. He said that if Ms Patterson's blood was on his jacket then it must have been planted there by police. He said that he did not have anything to do with Ms Patterson after 12 April 1999, when he cancelled an appointment to see her about his gambling problem.

Dupas said he did not contact Ms Patterson on 19 April, the day she was murdered, or go anywhere near her house. He said that he only left his Pascoe Vale home on that day to buy milk and petrol, do some shopping and pick up his de facto wife, and that while he was at home he was washing clothes and other gear in readiness for a camping trip, and working on a cocktail cabinet in his shed.

David Brustman, acting for Dupas, told the court that there were issues about how his client's jacket came to have blood on it and about whether or not the jacket proved anything. He said there was no argument about the fact that 13 stains had Ms Patterson's blood and the 14th had a combination of her blood and that of Mr Dupas.

'On the face of it, game, set and match,' Mr Brustman told the jury. He went on to try to suggest that Dupas was being framed, and that someone else had committed the murder.

In cross-examining Dupas, prosecutor Geoff Horgan pointed out that it must have been an amazing coincidence that out of all the jackets Dupas had in his home the police sprinkled the deceased's blood on the one he was wearing the day she was killed. Mr Horgan suggested that if this were the case then the police must have carried around a phial of Nicole Patterson's uncongealed blood for two days in order to sprinkle it on the jacket on the day he was arrested.

On 17 August 2000, after two and a half hours of deliberation, the jury returned a verdict of guilty. At Dupas's sentencing hearing, on 23 August 2000, Justice Vincent told him: 'I note that you have an appalling criminality history, involving repeated acts of sexual violence, and which extends over approximately 30 years. You have admitted 16 prior convictions involving six court appearances between 27 March 1972 and 11 November 1994.

'All of the offences were sexually related or motivated. A number of them involved physical violence and the use of a knife. On three separate occasions you were sentenced to terms of imprisonment for the commission of rape, aggravated assault or assault with intent to rape.

'On the second and third of these occasions, you committed your offences within a very short time of your release from custody. It appears that the only periods during which you were at large in the community without committing offences were two periods of approximately 12 months each during which you were subject to strict parole conditions — following your release from prison in 1992 and 1996.

'However, it was not long after that form of control was lifted by the expiration of the sentence to which it was related that you reverted to your usual type of criminal behaviour.

'You regarded Nicole Patterson as nothing more than prey to be entrapped and killed. Her life, youth and personal qualities assumed importance in your mind only by reason of the sense of satisfaction and power you experienced in taking them from her.

'At a fundamental level, as human beings, you present for us the awful, threatening and unanswerable question — how did you come to be as you are?'

Justice Frank Vincent sentenced Peter Norris Dupas to be imprisoned for the rest of his natural life without the opportunity for release on parole.

Peter Dupas has since been questioned about the unsolved murders of Margaret Maher, Mersina Halvagis, Helen McMahon and Kathleen Downes. He has denied involvement in any of them.

Chapter 9

MR SQUEAKY

Leonard John Fraser

Before he was sent to prison for the rest of his life on 7 September 2000, for the abduction, rape and murder of a 9-year-old girl, Leonard Fraser had spent almost 20 of the preceding 22 years behind bars for a series of rapes.

While in prison awaiting the trial that led to that last conviction, Fraser confessed to four more killings and took police to where the remains of some of his victims were concealed. His subsequent murder trial caused a worldwide sensation when one of his alleged victims, a 14-year-old schoolgirl, turned up alive and well — and now 18 years old — in the middle of proceedings.

Leonard John Fraser was born in the sugar-growing community of Ingham, North Queensland, on 27 June 1951. He was the second youngest of four children. When he was 6, his family packed up and moved to a brick house in Mt Druitt, one of the blue-collar outer western suburbs of Sydney.

According to court psychiatrists many years later, there was not the slightest indication in young Lenny's early childhood that he would grow up to be a vicious rapist and killer. While his upbringing, childhood and his environment appeared to have been normal, his schoolwork was poor. By the time he dropped out of high school in his second year there, at age 14, Lenny Fraser had learned to read but had learned little else, and had trouble writing his own name.

At the age of 15, Fraser was sentenced to 12 months in the Gosford Boys Home for stealing. Soon after his release, he received a two-year bond for assaulting a railway guard. Further convictions for driving without a licence, offensive behaviour and stealing cars culminated in 12 months' 'hard labour'.

Out of jail a mere 6 months later, Fraser was found guilty of transporting stolen goods interstate — into Queensland — which earned him two years' probation. Five weeks later he was sentenced to 2 weeks in jail in Townsville for stealing. In Sydney in 1972 he was fined $100 for living off the earnings of prostitution and later the same year was sentenced to five years' hard labour in Long Bay jail for a string of robberies.

But what investigators didn't know — and wouldn't find out until almost two years later — was that two months earlier, Fraser had raped a French woman in Sydney's Botanical Gardens. It was the first of what would be many rapes.

At 10 o'clock on the morning of 11 July 1974, just three weeks after he had been released from Long Bay, Fraser approached a young woman as she walked along a road in the Sydney outer western suburb of St Marys and attacked her from behind. Using what would become his 'calling card', Fraser twisted the woman's arm up behind her back and forced her down an embankment, where he raped her. Under the delusion that the woman had enjoyed what he had done, Fraser then walked his victim, hand-in-hand, back up onto the roadway before taking off.

Six days later, at 9 pm on 17 July, Fraser assaulted a 20-year-old woman who was working alone in a Mt Druitt dry-cleaning shop. Fraser followed her behind the counter when she went to look for his dry-cleaning — he did not in fact have any dry-cleaning there — and twisted her hand up behind her back. He was about to rape her when he was interrupted by other customers entering the shop. He fled.

Three days later, at Rooty Hill, another suburb in the same area, Fraser spoke briefly to a woman as she walked along a quiet road, then punched her in the face and forced her arm up her back. As the couple struggled towards a small creek, the woman remained calm and talked to her attacker. She convinced him that she was indeed in the mood for sex and would gladly submit, and suggested that they go back to Fraser's house and do it in his bed.

Fraser walked the woman, hand-in-hand, back up onto the road, just as he had done with the woman at St Marys. As soon as she saw her chance she broke free and fled to the nearest house, where she raised the alarm. Fraser wasn't hard to find — he had left his wallet, with his birth certificate in it, at the scene of the previous attack, in the dry-cleaning shop. He was quickly located and taken into custody.

Fraser confessed to one rape and the two attempted rapes. He denied that he would have had to force the woman in the dry-cleaning shop to have sex with him if they had not been disturbed. 'I would not have had to force her,' he told investigators. 'She was just about to come across.'

And then, much to the surprise of police, Fraser confessed to the rape in the Botanical Gardens, in the heart of Sydney and in broad daylight, almost 2 years earlier. The victim was a 37-year-old French tourist, who, along with her accountant husband and their two infant daughters, were visiting Sydney for an accountants' convention.

The attack took place as the woman was walking through the Sydney Botanical Gardens at 10 am. She had been planning to take some pictures of the Conservatorium of Music and then meet up with her husband and daughters. As she passed by some banana trees a man emerged from the shadows, put his arm around her neck from behind, punched her in the face many times with his other hand, dragged her into the undergrowth around the banana trees and raped her.

When he was interrupted by passers-by, the rapist took off with the woman's handbag, leaving his victim in a serious condition — she was semi-conscious, had multiple fractures to the face and was in severe shock.

Fraser told investigators that he was glad to have the crime off his chest at last. 'I don't know what came over me ... I have always regretted it,' he said. He told police that he had had an argument with his flatmate at their Kings Cross residence and he had gone to the Botanical Gardens, where he wandered around for a while until he targeted the French woman and attacked her.

When interviewed by a psychiatrist in Long Bay jail, Fraser said that at the time of the rape of the French woman he had been living off the proceeds of several prostitutes who worked the streets of Kings Cross, and was handing the bulk of the proceeds over to a 'minder'. Fraser claimed to have been involved in numerous homosexual relationships, but said that he had not been involved sexually with any of his 'workers'.

Fraser also told the psychiatrist that he would be happy if he never saw his siblings again, and that he hated his father and mother. His main ambition was to become a member of the Hell's Angels motorbike gang, he said.

In December 1974, at the Sydney District Court, Leonard Fraser pleaded guilty to two counts of rape and two counts of attempted rape. The court psychiatrist's disturbing assessment was that Fraser was beyond help: 'He has no conscience at all. He will use anyone and anything to his advantage without giving a lot of thought to other people's feelings. He has little or no impulse control. Apart from this there is no real psychiatric disability. There is no known treatment for this type of psychopathic state.'

With all of this in mind, Justice Wootten sent Fraser to prison for the maximum of 22 years and — reluctantly — set the non-parole period at what the law demanded: seven years. 'But I wish to make it clear in doing so that I am not in any way suggesting that you should be released at the end of the period,' Justice Wootten added.

The happiest person in the court when the sentence was handed down was Fraser's mother, Daphne, who spoke to a reporter from the *Sydney Morning Herald*. 'I have abandoned him as my son,' she said. 'I know it is a terrible thing to say, but I can rest when he is inside. I go to bed at night. And when I hear news of an assault or robbery, I know it will not be Lennie.'

Released in 1981 after serving the minimum seven years, Fraser made his way to Mackay, in Queensland,

and took a job as a labourer on the railways. He was soon back to his old ways. In 1982 Fraser gained entry to a woman's house by showing interest in a car she had for sale; once inside, he grabbed her from behind and held her arm up her back, as he had done in his previous attacks. To the amazement of investigating officers, the woman said that she talked Fraser into allowing her to ring her husband while the assault was taking place. During the call, Fraser took the phone and told the man: 'I hope you're not going to kill me. I just wanted to prove a point that somebody could break in and rape your missus.' In the Mackay District Court, Fraser was sentenced to two months in jail for aggravated assault on the woman.

When he was released from jail this time, Fraser stayed in Mackay, and by late that same year he was living with a woman and her son in an old house that had been converted into flats. He had a daughter with the woman and managed to hold down his job as a labourer with the railways for the next two and a half years.

In late 1985, after stalking a 21-year-old woman for several days as she went on her daily walks at an isolated beach at Shoal Point, north of Mackay, Fraser brutally raped her, again by attacking her from behind and holding her arm up her back, and again in broad daylight.

Given his record and the modus operandi used in the assault, the offender wasn't hard to find. This time he was sentenced to 12 years in jail. In sentencing Fraser, Justice Derrington said he regarded the prisoner as a dangerous man who preyed on women who were strangers and alone. 'They [the victims] would regard you as being the equivalent of a filthy animal,' he said. 'It [rape] is one of the worst forms of degradation on another human being you can think of, and it deserves no sympathy whatever.'

In Rockhampton's Etna Creek Prison, where Fraser served his time, he became known as 'Lenny the Loon' because of his erratic and unpredictable behaviour. His violent outbursts seemed to have no trigger, no reason, and the prison lore was that it was wise to give Lenny the widest possible berth.

The jail management team made sure that Fraser served out every day of his 12 years — they believed that the minute he was let out he would re-offend.

Fraser was released in January 1997. He soon moved in with a terminally ill woman who lived at Yeppoon, a coastal township south of Mackay. She had corresponded with him and visited him regularly while he was in prison, and he had told her that he was friendless, broke, and had nowhere to live.

The relationship developed into a sexual one, but Fraser became more and more aggressive. When the woman left the home to go to Brisbane for cancer treatment, Fraser followed, and after she refused to come home with him, he allegedly raped her in the hospital chapel. The woman died six months later of her cancer.

Fraser then went to live in Mount Morgan, a mining town of 3500 residents on the Burnett Highway southwest of Yeppoon and Rockhampton. It didn't take long before the locals were talking about the strange man who had come to live in their quiet little hamlet.

An intellectually disabled woman complained to police that Fraser had annoyed her while she was riding on a bus. Fraser was seen roaming around the town at all hours of the night, and every day when the local school came out he was waiting at the front gate, and would try to strike up a conversation with any female, irrespective of age, who passed in or out.

Fraser frequented employment agencies that serviced the intellectually handicapped, in search of female partners, and he mowed lawns and drove children to school for petrol and beer money. Towards the end of 1998, he moved into a flat in Rockhampton with intellectually handicapped 19-year-old Cristine Wraight.

By early April 1999, another woman and her 11-year-old daughter had moved into the spare room in the flat to help pay the rent. But it didn't last long. Soon the woman moved out, after accusing Fraser of interfering with her daughter.

Fraser was kicked out when the landlady caught him having sex with Wraight's blue heeler cattle dog in the backyard. The dog died several weeks later from rat poison.

On 22 April 1999, 9-year-old Keyra Steinhardt disappeared when she was taking a shortcut through a vacant allotment on her way home from school. An eyewitness to the abduction, Lynette Kiernan, who lived opposite the vacant allotment, told police that she saw a man catch up with the little girl and hit her from behind in the head area. The child fell to the ground. Ms Kiernan couldn't see her in the long grass, but she saw her assailant fall on the girl and move as if he was raping her.

Then the assailant ran away. He returned shortly afterwards in a car, lifted the little girl from the ground into the boot and drove away. Terrified of repercussions, it took Ms Kiernan a critical 20 minutes to pluck up the courage to make an anonymous phone call to the police. But by then, little Keyra was dead and disposed of.

The following day police picked up Fraser — Ms Kiernan's description of his early model red Mazda 626 sedan had led them straight to him. It was two weeks before he broke and confessed to Keyra's murder and took police to her naked body. He had placed it on a thick bed of grass near the Rockhampton racecourse. Her throat had been cut and, as if in a belated veil of chastity, Fraser had draped Keyra's green school jumper over her torso.

When questioned by investigators, Fraser's flatmate, Ms Wraight, said that she had gone for a drive with Fraser along a bush track near Rockhampton's racecourse on the day that Keyra had gone missing, and that at one point Fraser had stopped the car and told her not to watch what he was doing.

She said he removed what looked like a blonde doll wearing a green school uniform from the boot. Ms Wraight said that when Fraser saw her looking, he dropped what he was carrying, came back to the car, reached into the window and punched her. She then looked straight ahead, and after a little while Fraser got back into the car and they drove away. Ms Wraight said that when they returned home that evening, Fraser washed the boot out thoroughly.

DNA samples taken from the blood and hair found in the boot of Fraser's car matched that of Keyra Steinhardt. There was also another female's blood on the boot hinge and on a cigarette paper in the glove box. On 7 May, Fraser was charged with the abduction, rape and murder of Keyra Steinhardt.

In September 2000, prosecutor Paul Rutledge suggested to the Brisbane Supreme Court that Fraser, who had pleaded not guilty to the charges, had attacked the little girl for no reason other than sexual gratification. Mr Rutledge put it to the court: 'Why did he [Fraser] follow a 9–year–old into the allotment and hit her so hard she dropped to the ground? Why did he strip her naked?' (Due to the advanced decomposition of Keyra's body, it had been impossible to determine exactly how she died or whether or not she had been sexually assaulted.)

Ms Kiernan, who had seen the assault from her house, told the court that she had seen Fraser standing next to Keyra at the traffic lights the day before the little girl was murdered.

And there was more evidence. Mr Rutledge noted a damning tape recording — of a conversation that Fraser had had in the Rockhampton watchhouse, in which he had asked another prisoner to dispose of a knife he had hidden in a peg box in his apartment. Mr Rutledge told the court that that knife was the one that Fraser plunged into the neck and upper body of the little girl.

Adding what seemed an extra twist of pain for Keyra's family, the court heard that it had only been two weeks before her death that Keyra had first been allowed to walk the 30–minute route from her family's North Rockhampton home to school by herself. She had been excited by this new freedom, and on the day of her death had left her friends outside the school gate to make her way home alone.

Fraser remained silent throughout the trial. He gave no evidence on his own behalf except to steadfastly deny at the start that he had abducted, raped or murdered Keyra, or that he was in or near the allotment on the day in question.

Yet when police had charged Fraser with the crimes, he had offered an apology to Keyra's parents. 'I'd like to say to her mother and father, and I know a lot of people won't believe me, but if you check my background, it's not my go to harm a child,' he had said. 'I'm just sorry this is happening, and I don't know what made me do it; at least I can try to ... I'm going to try and get help after I get sentenced and all, so that's a good step.'

Leonard Fraser was found guilty of the abduction and murder of Keyra Steinhardt at Rockhampton on 22 April 1999. At Fraser's sentencing, on 9 November 2000, Justice Ken Mackenzie labelled him a sexual predator of the worst kind: 'The offence involved severe, indeed extreme, violence on a child.'

Justice Mackenzie said that he had no reason to suppose that Fraser had any prospect of rehabilitation, and sentenced him to an indefinite life sentence. Under Queensland legislation enacted in 1997, an indefinite life sentence is different from a life sentence. With a life sentence, a prisoner can automatically apply for parole after 15 years; with an indefinite life sentence he or she must apply not only to the Parole Board but also to a Supreme Court judge to be released, and both have to be satisfied that the person no longer poses a threat to the community before the indefinite order is lifted. This sentence virtually slammed the cell door on Fraser for the rest of his life.

But that was not to be the end of it. Police had very good reason to believe that Fraser had also murdered another schoolgirl, Natasha Ryan, and three women, Julie Turner, Bev Leggo and Sylvia Benedetti, all of whom had gone missing in Rockhampton between September 1998 and April 1999.

Natasha Ryan, 14, had disappeared on 2 September 1998, while on her way to a north Rockhampton school — in the same area where Keyra Steinhardt was killed.

Julie Dawn Turner, 39, had worked with Fraser for a couple of months in 1998 at the Rockhampton abattoirs. On 28 December 1998 Julie left Rockhampton's Airport Liberty Nightclub in the early hours of the morning in an intoxicated state. Apparently broke, she had asked around for enough money to get a cab home, and when none was forthcoming she had started walking. From there she disappeared. Julie had previously told friends that she was moving in with a guy named 'Lenny', but hadn't said anything more about him.

Beverly Doreen Leggo, 36, had met Fraser at a Mount Morgan hostel he was staying at in 1997. Ms Leggo was last seen on 1 March 1999, at a bank in the CBD, near the East Street Mall.

Sylvia Maria Benedetti, 19, disappeared on 17 April 1999. Six days later, while police were searching for Keyra Steinhardt, who had disappeared the day before, they were led to the derelict Queensland Hotel by the men who had been employed to wreck it. The wreckers had made a horrific discovery. In room 13 the carpet was soggy with blood and there was blood sprayed all over the ceiling and walls. There were bone fragments in the carpet. In a downstairs disconnected freezer police found a pair of women's shoes submerged in filthy water.

A forensic examination confirmed that the blood was human. Police believed that the blood was Sylvia Benedetti's. And given the number of women who had gone missing in recent months, they were also beginning to suspect that there was a serial killer in their midst.

The attack had been so savage that the victim had lost about 4 litres of blood. This was a very high proportion of the blood a person would have in their body — the average person has 5 to 7 litres. Police believed that Sylvia Benedetti was known to Fraser, that she had been seen with him on the night before she disappeared. DNA tests of blood found in the boot of Fraser's car showed that it matched the blood found in room 13.

But while police believed that Fraser had murdered all four women, without their bodies or a confession they couldn't pin a thing on him. Not until he started talking to his cellmate, Allen Quinn, that is. 'What I have gone through has caused me to kill these people,' he allegedly told the cellmate. 'All the hate over the years came to the fore and ended with the murder of the people.'

When confronted by detectives about these confessions, Fraser shocked them by offering to take them to where the bodies were concealed. In a top-secret operation that could have fallen apart at any time — Fraser said that he 'hated the media and did not want any coverage' — homicide detectives took him out of prison and flew him on the Premier's private jet to Rockhampton. They secretly videotaped him as he led them to the remains of Ms Leggo and Ms Turner.

Partial remains of Sylvia Benedetti had already been discovered in bushland near Sandy Point Beach by surfers. Fraser now led police to the rest of the remains. With this evidence, detectives charged Fraser with the four murders.

At his trial in the Brisbane Supreme Court in April 2003, before Justice Brian Ambrose, Fraser pleaded not guilty to the murders of Natasha Ryan, Julie Turner, Bev Leggo and Sylvia Benedetti.

The jury was told by prosecutor Paul Rutledge that Fraser had boasted to his cellmate that he had killed Natasha Ryan by knifing her because she was pregnant to him. He said he had then placed her body in a grave he had dug on a property outside Rockhampton.

Fraser had also said that he murdered Sylvia Benedetti, and 'bled her like an animal', in a disused hotel. He had made a bloodied hand mark on the wall and then smeared over it, he said. Fraser also said that he had followed Julie Turner from the Rockhampton nightclub and attacked her when she stopped to have a cigarette.

In the secret videotape recorded on the day Fraser took detectives to the victims' bodies, the court heard Fraser say, when he showed them where Ms Leggo's body was buried, at Nankin Creek, 20 km outside Rockhampton, that he couldn't remember whose body it was because his mind had become 'scrambled', but that it didn't matter because he was going to spend the rest of his life in jail anyway.

The court heard that Sylvia Benedetti was last seen on 18 April 1999, sitting in the Rockhampton City

Mall with Fraser. It was her blood that had been found in Fraser's car with that of Keyra Steinhardt, and it was her blood that was splattered all over the hotel room.

A man who owned a shop opposite the Queensland Hotel told the court that he had mentioned to Fraser on 21 April 1999 that the hotel was about to be demolished. Fraser had become angry and red in the face, the man remembered, and had clenched his fists and said, 'They can't do that.' Two days later the wreckers discovered the blood-soaked room.

On Thursday, 10 April 2003, the case took a sensational turn when one of the alleged victims, 18-year-old Natasha Ryan, was discovered by police hiding in a cupboard at the home of her boyfriend, 26-year-old Scott Black, a kilometre from her mother's home in Rockhampton. Police said that they had acted on a tip-off arising from the trial.

But despite the media's frenzy for the story, they were given no explanation for Natasha Ryan's disappearance and re-emergence four and a half years later. The story was to be sold to the highest bidder — and the deal was being brokered by celebrity Sydney public relations agent Max Markson, who flew to Rockhampton to make sure his latest acquisition remained under tight wraps.

Now living back with her bewildered mother, it was rumoured that Natasha Ryan wanted $250,000 for her story. All her father, Robert Ryan, who was separated from Natasha's mother, said to the local press was that after believing his daughter to be dead for all that time, 'I couldn't stop cuddling her. It was like I saw a ghost.'

The detective in charge of the case, Detective Senior Sergeant David Hickey, told Fraser's lawyer,

Adrian Gundelach, that when Natasha Ryan went missing in 1998 they had searched Mr Black's home but couldn't come up with the slightest indication that a female lived there.

Detective Hickey said that a surveillance team had been assigned to watch Mr Black's house, and to observe his comings and goings and the people he associated with, but that there had been nothing whatever to connect him with the disappearance of Natasha Ryan.

Detective Hickey did not indicate whether or not any charges would be laid against Natasha Ryan or Scott Black.

The court immediately declared Fraser not guilty of Natasha Ryan's murder, and his lawyers applied to have the whole trial declared a mistrial. The court was then adjourned so that the judge could consider the question.

Much to the relief of the victims' parents, after a four-day adjournment, Justice Ambrose ruled that the trial would continue. Mr Gundelach indicated immediately that he intended to call Ms Ryan as a witness when the occasion arose.

When the trial resumed, on 15 April 2003, the jury heard evidence from Allen Quinn, Fraser's former cellmate. He said that Fraser often boasted to the other inmates, saying, 'They're trying to get me on these murders, but they won't be able to pin them on me.'

Quinn went on to say that Fraser had confessed to him that he had killed Natasha Ryan, saying that the murder weapon, a knife, would never be found. Fraser said that Ms Ryan had asked him for a lift to the beachside township of Yeppoon, and that he had knocked her out after she'd fallen asleep on his shoulder in the car (to make sure she would not wake up in a hurry). Fraser had also said that he had disposed of Natasha's body underneath a mango tree and that the body had been removed by a mystery man named Casper, who had taken it to Yamba.

But that was just one of a multitude of lies among the truths that Fraser had told Quinn, who was relaying all Fraser's statements to the police. They checked out every one. Another of Fraser's fantasies was that he had murdered a female backpacker and dumped her body in a crocodile pond in an abandoned wildlife park north of Rockhampton. Only after police had dug up the pond and searched the farm extensively did they put that one down as a hoax.

Quinn said that Fraser also boasted about how he drove his ute past a police car in Rockhampton when he had the body of one of his victims, Julie Turner, in the back, covered with a tarpaulin. Fraser also said that he had used the ute before.

Because of all the information they were receiving from Quinn, police had decided to install a listening device in his and Fraser's cell. This allowed them to record Fraser telling Quinn about murdering Beverly Leggo after he had taken her for a swim at Nankin Creek, outside Rockhampton. 'I smashed her across the jaw ... she was semi-conscious. I pulled the rope that is used for a swing ... over and put it around her neck twice and tucked the end through the loops and pulled it tight.'

Fraser then laughed as he went on: 'You should have seen her kick when I let the rope go. I heard her neck break — and then she stopped kicking and her legs dangled in the water. It didn't take much to kill her, because she was really skinny. I took the rope off her and dragged her through the waterhole into the long grass, where I put her on that ditch. I made sure that I pulled the tall grass back up as I went so there was no trail left behind in the grass.

'To make sure she was dead I placed her black sporting briefs around her neck and pulled them tight, so if she woke up she wouldn't breathe, she would die.'

The tape also recorded Fraser telling how he had met Sylvia Benedetti, on 18 April 1999, in the Rockhampton Mall. At the time, she was unhappy with where she was living and was going through a bad time with her boyfriend.

'I took Benedetti to a disused hotel — to room 13. I told her that I had drugs stored there. I tried to kiss her — she didn't like it. I hit her and knocked her out. I went downstairs to check if anyone had heard her scream.

'I went back upstairs and she was just lying there staring at me. When they are unconscious they always stare at you. I knew I was going to be in trouble. So I picked up a block of wood. I thought that it was a block of wood. It could have been a window counterweight, I don't know ... but it had serrated edges.'

Natasha Ryan, who had by now sold her story to the TV program *60 Minutes* and to *Woman's Day* magazine for an undisclosed sum, appeared in court as a defence witness. She told a packed gallery that she had never seen Fraser before in her life. She said that her mother had dropped her off at school on 31 August 1998 and that she had got into trouble that day with a teacher. She had felt that that was the last straw, and had decided to run away and stay with Mr Black. She had been with him ever since.

According to the police investigation into her disappearance, the last time Natasha had been seen by anyone was when two friends saw her near a Rockhampton cinema several days after her disappearance.

As the trial drew to a close it was revealed by the prosecution that Fraser had sent police a 'press release' from a 'Mr Squeaky', in an attempt to throw them off the trail. 'I want you to understand that I am responsible for all the murders in the Rockhampton area,' Mr Squeaky said in the 'press release', which was produced by Fraser in prison on 18 January 2001, three weeks after he had led police to the graves of three of his victims. 'You will never know my real name, you can refer to me as Squeaky,' it continued. Unbeknown to Fraser, however, by this time detectives were recording all his and Quinn's conversations through the listening device in their cell.

Mr Squeaky's press release said the information it contained about the murders was only known to him. Fraser's Mr Squeaky plan failed miserably because of the recordings of conversations in the two men's cell, and because the press release contained information that only the killer knew — some of it, even the police did not know.

One of these pieces of information was that Beverly Leggo had been strangled with her black panties and a bra. The admission was made 3 days before forensic tests revealed that that was how she had died.

Mr Squeaky also said that when Julie Turner had been murdered, he had left her sandals near a particular electrical box. A subsequent search in that area found one of the sandals and Ms Turner's bra.

In the press release, Mr Squeaky also admitted to committing many other crimes in the Rockhampton district, including many rapes that had never been reported to the police.

All Fraser had done by creating the Mr Squeaky press release, the prosecution noted, was incriminate himself further.

On 9 May 2003, after a little more than a day's deliberation, the jury convicted Fraser of the murders of Sylvia Benedetti and Beverly Doreen Leggo, and the manslaughter of Julie Dawn Turner.

The verdict of manslaughter meant that the jury believed that Fraser did not intend to kill Julie Turner. Fraser stood silent in the dock, then yawned and stretched his hands behind his head, as the verdicts were handed down.

On 28 May 2003, Fraser lodged an appeal against his conviction for the killings. At the time of going to press, this appeal had not yet been heard.

On 13 June 2003, Justice Brian Ambrose sentenced Leonard John Fraser to three indefinite jail terms for the two murders and one manslaughter, and described Fraser as an 'untreatable psychopath' with a brutal sexual desire — for any females from middle-aged women down to children.

Justice Ambrose said that Fraser would not be eligible for parole, which was all but impossible anyway, until he was 81. Even then, should he live as long as that, the most likely scenario was that he would die in jail.

Chapter 10

LEFT FOR DEAD

Ian Craig Styman
and Peter David Taber

When Phillip Reeves, proprietor of the local grocery store, found 71-year-old Joy Alchin's body on the bedroom floor of her secluded Spies Avenue home at Greenwell Point, on the Friday afternoon of 19 January 2001, police estimated that she could have been dead for up to two days. They turned out to be very wrong.

The elderly lady, who weighed a mere 50 kg and was 149 cm tall, had been gagged with her own underwear; her hands and feet had been trussed with cable ties and duct tape; her head was inside a pillow case which was tied at the neck; and she was tied to the bed. Mrs Alchin had bruises and cuts to her face and body, swollen lips, and bruising consistent with sexual assault. Her small fibro home had been ransacked.

At news of this atrocity, residents of the tiny coastal township went into shock. Greenwell Point is a relaxed two-hour drive along the coast road south of Sydney, and has a population of 1000 — it increases to 2000 in the holiday season. A murder in this close-knit hamlet was inconceivable.

Mrs Alchin had lived in Greenwell Point for about 15 years, and had spent most of her life in the district.

'This is the last place you would expect something like this to happen,' the local real estate agent told the press. 'People around here leave their cars and their houses unlocked. There's virtually no crime here except in the holidays, when there's more people around.'

For almost two months the assault and murder of Joy Alchin remained a mystery. And then, on 19 March, acting on a tip-off, police raided two homes in Brisbane and arrested Shannon Troy Styman, 22, his uncle, Ian Craig Styman, 37, Peter David Taber, 27, and Mrs Alchin's niece, 19-year-old Leonie Kaye Ravell. They had been in hiding there for the previous two months.

Extradited to Sydney, the men were charged with murder and Leonie Ravell was charged with being an accessory after the offence. Only after the charges had been laid was it revealed to the press that on the night of the murder an anonymous caller had rung 000 and said that an elderly lady had been assaulted and was tied, still alive, to a bed.

The call had been treated as a hoax, and the information had never been passed on to the police. The police admitted that if they had received the call, Mrs Alchin might have been found alive. Instead it took her up to 10 days to die a slow, agonising death from dehydration and suffocation.

Mrs Alchin's only daughter, Joanne Rutter, who lived in Wagga Wagga, in southwestern New South Wales, said she could not forgive the operator who had dismissed the call as a prank. Had the call been passed on to police as it should have been, Mrs Rutter said, she might have received a call to visit her mother in the hospital rather than in the morgue.

The prisoners, who had all been remanded in custody, were arraigned, and their committal hearing began in the Sydney Central Local Court on 19 February 2002. When asked about how long it would have taken Mrs Alchin to die and the cause of death, Dr Peter Bradhurst, of the NSW Institute of Forensic Medicine, told the court that when he examined Mrs Alchin's body, the nasal passage did not appear to have been completely blocked but the mouth was. He had not had the opportunity to examine the fabric of the pillowslip which had been placed over Mrs Alchin's head, but conceded that she may have been able to breathe through it.

Dr Bradhurst said that if the mouth and nose had been blocked, death would have occurred in five to ten minutes, and the cause would be smothering, but because it had been demonstrated that Mrs Alchin could have breathed through her nose, he had instead concluded that she had died of asphyxiation. Dr Bradhurst said that with increasing dehydration — the mean room temperature in the house in summer was 25°C — Mrs Alchin would have lapsed into a coma or become unconscious, and at that stage she would have been unable to get sufficient oxygen to breathe. He concluded that while it was possible that she had died before 16 January, it was most probable that Mrs Alchin had died between 16 January and 18 January — up to 12 days after she had been attacked.

The court was told that it was common knowledge that Mrs Alchin kept paper bags full of old and new $100 bills in her house, and that family members had often borrowed money from her over the years.

The prosecution alleged that one of the accused, Leonie Ravell, had made it known to the three other accused that there was a lot of money in her aunt's house, and that the men had gone to the house on Ravell's instigation and tortured the old woman until she told them where the money was.

Ian Styman and Peter Taber were committed to stand trial for murder, robbery with deprivation of liberty in aggravated circumstances, and sexual assault. Both pleaded not guilty when proceedings began on 8 September 2002 in the Supreme Court, before Justice Graham Barr.

Shannon Styman pleaded not guilty to identical charges of murder and sexual assault. He pleaded guilty to robbing Mrs Alchin and depriving her of her liberty in aggravated circumstances and in company, but refused to name any accomplices.

In his opening address to the jury, Crown prosecutor John Kiely, SC, said that the evidence against the charged men was very strong. He said that Mrs Alchin was murdered by the Stymans and Taber through reckless indifference to human life.

Mr Kiely said that the defendants had gone as far as to ask a man who worked part-time for the police to tamper with DNA evidence. Ian Styman, accompanied by his nephew Shannon, was alleged to have approached Ian's brother John, who worked with the Nowra police. Both had had a cheek swab taken and appeared very concerned about the results.

'If they come back positive, you're in the shit,' John Styman was alleged to have said to Ian, Mr Kiely told the court. Ian then allegedly asked John: 'Any way of getting the results before they get back? Do you think you can change the results?' John was alleged to have replied: 'There's no way in the world. I don't want anything to do with it.'

The court then heard a little about Mrs Alchin. Joy Golbey Alchin was born on 28 November 1930, had three sisters (two of whom lived at Greenwell Point), had been married and divorced, and had one daughter. She lived alone in her tiny fibro house, was in excellent health and had no pets — her sole companion was her religion. All the locals who had dealings with her said that she was a kindly old lady who kept to herself. May Batchelor, who lived next door to Mrs Alchin, said she had only spoken to her neighbour once in the previous three years.

'You would never see her [Mrs Alchin]', said the local newsagent. 'She used to order her groceries on the Wednesday and have them delivered on the Friday, and she always paid cash. She was a lovely lady to talk to on the phone and when she paid for the groceries.' Apart from tradespeople, she had little to do with the other residents of Greenwell Point.

By all accounts, while she was pleasant enough, Mrs Alchin did not suffer fools gladly, and could also be very abrasive, easily putting people off. This seemed to be the case with her own family. And she hadn't seemed to care too much about it; she was very much her own woman.

Mrs Alchin had a bit of money of her own plus some she had inherited from a good friend who had died and left no dependants. Around 1987 Mrs Alchin began drawing her money out of the bank in $100 notes and hoarding it in the house. This was rather odd, given that she hardly spent any money on anything: her only luxuries were the occasional confectionery or iced treat.

At the start of the trial the court heard about a call made to the emergency number that could have saved

Mrs Alchin's life. Police alleged that Ian Styman rang 000 — the call went through to the Warilla Communication Centre — at 4.54 am on 7 January 2001. Operator Anne Maher took the call. This is the transcript of that call:

Caller (Voice 1): Hello.

Emergency Operator Anne Maher (Voice 2): Hello.

V1: Could you send a car out please?

V2: Where to?

V1: Spies.

V2: Where?

V1: Spies Avenue, Greenwell Point.

V2: What's happening there?

V1: There was a couple of blokes that went in with guns, second from the house from the corner.

V2: What do you mean ... a couple of blokes went in?

V1: That went in the house, there's a little old lady there ...

V2: Break and enter?

V1: I can't talk but they're, they're here.

V2: What ... what number?

The call was then terminated by the caller.

The court heard that Ms Maher did not enter the details of the call into the Computer Incident Dispatch System (CIDS). Had she done so, the police would have sent a car to Spies Avenue immediately. Instead, Ms Maher expected to talk to a police officer she had been talking to earlier.

Ms Maher told the court that the emergency call dropped in over the top of a call she was making to

Cooma police, and that she thought the call had come through to her by mistake. She thought this had happened because a mechanical malfunction had diverted the call to her.

Unsure about what to do about the call, she had consulted her supervisor and said in court that she had not entered the call into CIDS because she had been instructed not to. A four and a half minute delay on the master tapes suggested that she had followed guidelines to the letter: she had approached her supervisor, Acting Sergeant George Stewart, about what form of action to take and had followed his instructions.

'I have strong work ethics. I don't recall the call, I don't recall anything ... I sought advice from my supervisor. Why would I not?' she told the court.

'In that job you can't assume anything, you take everything very seriously. If I was unsure of anything, I would seek advice from my supervisor and that's what I did. I followed standard procedure. If I didn't do a CIDS job, it was because I was instructed not to. I have to be unlucky, unlucky is my middle name.'

Ms Maher told the court that she had faced a departmental investigation over the incident, and at the time of an interview with police had felt suicidal and been suffering nightmares.

She broke down in tears and told the court, 'I was devastated.'

The court heard that a floor plan found in the home of one of the accused men had raised the suspicions of Mrs Alchin's sister, Cheryle Ravell. Mrs Ravell said that she found a sketch that 'looked similar' to the layout of her sister's house at Greenwell Point in an exercise book at the home shared by her daughter Leonie Ravell and one of the accused men, Peter Taber. The couple lived in South Nowra, not far from Greenwell Point.

A boarder at Taber's house, Donyelle Turner, 20, told the court that when she had returned home from a trip to Sydney on 16 January 2001 she had found several appliances in the house that she had never seen before — including a stereo system, a washing machine, a TV and a refrigerator — and a second-hand motor vehicle outside. She was so suspicious of her landlord's sudden good fortune that she sneaked into his bedroom to have a look around.

In the bedroom she found $900 in old-style $100 bills in Leonie Ravell's purse. Given that Taber had recently tried to borrow $2000 from her (Ms Turner) so that he and Leonie Ravell could go on a holiday, she wondered where the money had come from.

Ms Turner said that Taber had also recently asked Leonie's sister, Melinda Ravell, for a loan of $2000, without success. He had then suggested that they visit Leonie's aunt, Joy Alchin. Leonie had not wanted to go, but she and Taber had driven off. When they returned, they said that they had rung Mrs Alchin, but she had refused to lend them the money.

Ms Turner told the court that in a conversation she had heard before Christmas 2000, between Leonie Ravell and Peter Taber, Ravell had said: 'We can always kill her. It is not like anyone will notice she is missing.' Taber had said that they would never get away with it, but Ravell had said that they *would* get away with it, and that she and Melinda (Ravell) had planned it a long time ago.

The court then heard that car owner Alan Stoker had sold a soft-top Suzuki Sierra to Ian Styman on the afternoon of 7 January 2001, the day Joy Alchin had been tied up and left lying on her bedroom floor.

Mr Stoker, of the outer Sydney western suburb of Guildford, told the court that he had received a call about the car, which he had advertised as for sale in the paper, and that at about midday, Ian Styman, two other males and a woman had arrived to inspect the car. After a 10-minute test drive they had offered to pay $4300 for it, $900 below Mr Stoker's asking price.

Once Mr Stoker had accepted the offer, Styman had handed over a wad of cash, among it 10 old-style paper $100 notes. Styman had said that he was then going to nearby Parramatta to buy a CD player and a stereo.

The court also heard that a police search of Taber's residence had turned up rolls of duct tape similar to that used in Joy Alchin's assault in the bedroom, a bag of similar cable ties in the loungeroom, and screwed-up duct tape in the backyard and in the back of a ute. DNA tests made on blood found on the duct tape matched it with Mrs Alchin's blood.

The home also contained several almost new appliances: a free-standing fan, a Sony PlayStation, a sandwich-maker, a TV and a stereo — and the boxes they had been packed in. In the garage police found surgical gloves and Halloween masks.

Sarah Burgess, a checkout operator and workmate of Leonie Ravell, told the court that on 8 January 2001 Taber and Ravell went shopping at the Nowra Kmart and arrived at the checkout with two trolleys laden with household appliances — the total bill was about $1500. The full amount was paid in old $100 notes.

Ian Craig Styman and Peter David Taber

The court heard that when Taber was questioned by police on 24 January 2001, he had denied discussing killing Mrs Alchin with Ravell.

Taber had alleged that twice within the previous two years Mrs Alchin had lent money to members of her family and then used a lawyer to recall the loans. In 1999 she had lent $22,200 to her younger sister, Cheryle Ravell, and $23,000 to her niece, Melinda Green. Following a falling out with both Ms Ravell and Ms Green, Mrs Alchin had asked for her money back in October 2000. It was paid in full by both parties.

The court was told that Taber had told police he worked as a shed builder, and was very often paid large sums of cash. Quite often he worked for elderly people who paid him in cash in old notes, he said. And although his bank account showed very small balances, Taber said that over the previous 15 months he had had his 'hands on forty or fifty grand, probably a bit more'.

'I haven't got 40 or 50 grand sittin' around the house or a bank account or something like that,' he said. 'That's how much has gone through my books, roughly.'

Taber had admitted to police that he had pawned his tools at one stage, but said it was only a temporary measure, done while he was waiting for a cheque for $6000 to be cleared.

A record of interview with Ian Styman which was presented to the court revealed that he had been living on unemployment benefits when he spent $5100 on the car and a TV — the day after Joy Alchin was robbed and left for dead. Styman, who was married and had two children, received $407 in social security benefits a fortnight. The court heard that he made an average of $200 to $300 per week as a computer technician when he could find work, and that since the beginning of the previous year (2000) he had made about $8000 installing computer chips which enabled people to play pirate video games. However, Styman said there was probably only $20 in total in his four bank accounts and nothing in his wife's account.

Mr Kiely said that it was Styman who had made the 000 call at 4.54 am on 7 January. He went on to say that later on the day Styman bought the car and TV, and Taber bought a ute, and that the other accused, Styman's nephew, Shannon, paid $900 for a motorbike on the next day, 8 January — all these purchases were paid for in cash, and with old banknotes.

A friend of Ian Styman told police that late in December he had come across Taber practising tying up Styman in the loungeroom, and that he had then driven them to Greenwell Point late at night. They had allegedly tried to break into Mrs Alchin's home that night, but she woke up and they fled. The following day Mrs Alchin had new security doors fitted to her home.

When questioned in court about the crime itself, Taber tried to distance himself from it. He said that on the night of the murder he was at home playing a PlayStation computer game until the early hours of the morning. The game had been lent to him by Ian Styman, he said. He told the court that while he was playing the game Shannon Styman arrived at his house and told him that he (Styman) had just robbed a drug dealer. Taber claimed that Shannon Styman later changed his story: he had not robbed a drug dealer, but had robbed an old woman in her home. Taber told the court that Shannon told him he got $23,000 from the robbery, and then that Shannon gave him (Taber) and Ian Styman $5000 each.

Taber's de facto wife, Leonie Ravell, then told the court that she did not remember seeing Taber playing any computer games that day. Ravell said she went to bed at about 8 pm that night and Taber did not join her in the bedroom until the following day.

When Ian Styman took the stand he told the court that the first he knew of the crime was when his nephew, Shannon Styman, told him that he and his friend, Peter Taber, had 'done an old lady's place over'.

Styman denied that he and Taber had tied up Mrs Alchin, and that they had ransacked her house while Shannon kept an eye on Mrs Alchin. Styman said that on the night of the murder he was at home fixing a computer in his garage. He said he was cooking up something to eat at 3 am when he received a call from Taber telling him that Shannon had done something stupid and asking him to meet Taber right away.

Ian Styman's wife, Sharyn, told the court that her husband wasn't home that night.

When Shannon Styman took the stand, he told the court that he, his uncle (Ian Styman) and Peter Taber had broken into Mrs Alchin's house on the night of 6 January 2001 and had left the premises after about 20 minutes, as soon as they found the bag of money.

Shannon Styman said that Mrs Alchin didn't let out 'so much as a moan' when she was surprised by the three men in the early hours of the morning. They tied her hands and feet, gagged her with her own underwear and placed a pillow case over her head. He strenuously denied that Mrs Alchin had been bashed or sexually assaulted.

When asked by Mr Kiely if it appeared that Mrs Alchin had been unconscious throughout the ordeal, Shannon Styman replied that she had moved only slightly, but had been breathing all the while and offered no resistance in any way. In his opinion she had been completely passive.

Shannon Styman said it had taken about one minute to bind Mrs Alchin. He said that it had been his job to stay with her while the others ransacked the house. He said that Taber said to her: 'Just tell us where the money is.' He said that, because Taber made the demand after Mrs Alchin had been bound and gagged, it sounded a bit silly, but that was what took place.

Shannon Styman denied that Mrs Alchin could have been unconscious throughout the ordeal because she had been bashed, and said he had no idea how Mrs Alchin had sustained the injuries to her vaginal and rectal region.

Asked why it had been necessary for him to stay with Mrs Alchin while the others searched the house, Shannon Styman replied that it was so she wouldn't fall off the bed and hurt herself.

He told the court that when he asked Taber and Ian Styman if the old lady was going to be untied before they left, he was satisfied with the answer that they would ring 000 and help would arrive shortly after. 'I always had the belief that she would be let go. I did not think that she would die,' he said.

The court heard that when Shannon Styman hadn't heard anything about the home invasion on the radio in the following days, he had assumed that the police were conducting a 'quiet' investigation. 'I thought that if I rang the police they would catch me,' he said. 'When they found her it was too late, and I knew that I was in a lot of trouble. I felt guilty that I did rob the old lady and that she died.'

Shannon Styman told the court that he had checked that Mrs Alchin was breathing all right before they left the house. He said that Ian Styman had found $23,300 in cash in a bag beside Mrs Alchin's bed and the trio had returned to Taber's house and divided up the money: $14,000 to Taber, $7000 to Ian Styman and $2300 to him. He had the impression that $7000 of the money Taber took would go to Leonie Ravell.

The court was told by the prosecution that when Mrs Alchin was eventually found, she had curled her legs up beneath a table, and there was evidence that she had wriggled around the room — and that she had bruised herself — in desperate attempts to get free. However, she had been unable to do anything with her feet tied together and her hands tied behind her back; it seemed she had lain there for about 10 days, after which she had lapsed into a coma and died.

On 13 December 2002 Peter Taber and Ian Styman were found guilty of murder and aggravated break and enter for the purpose of committing a serious indictable offence. Shannon Styman was found guilty of manslaughter. All three were found not guilty of aggravated sexual intercourse without consent and of the alternative charge, sexual intercourse without consent.

A crowd of Mrs Alchin's friends, supporters and relatives, including her daughter, Joanne Rutter, were in the gallery to hear the verdict.

On 28 February 2002, in a packed Sydney Supreme Court, Justice Graham Barr sentenced Peter Taber and Ian Styman to life imprisonment without the possibility of parole. Shannon Styman was sentenced to 15 years with a minimum 10 years.

Leonie Ravell was given a two-year good behaviour bond for hindering police. A manslaughter charge against her had been dropped in exchange for her evidence.

'[Ian] Styman recruited his nephew, and the three strong young men broke into Mrs Alchin's home. Once there, they held down — in her own home — a sleeping woman they knew was alone and elderly and unlikely to have the strength to resist,' Justice Barr said.

'Then they stuffed her underpants in her mouth, wrapped it with duct tape, bound her ankles and tied her wrists behind her back with cable ties so tight they were embedded in her flesh. With a pillow case placed over her head and a sheet across her body, they left.

'Although they did not intend or desire Mrs Alchin to die, I think that their cool and callous indifference was as blameful as if they had,' Justice Barr told the court. 'Both Ian Styman and Peter Taber would have been aware of Mrs Alchin's fate when she was not rescued by emergency services.

'It took Mrs Alchin 10 days to die a long, lonely and painful death,' he said. 'Their level of culpability is so extreme that the community interest in retribution, punishment and deterrence can only be met by the imposition of a life sentence.'

Chapter 11

THE KILLER IN THE KITCHEN

Katherine Mary Knight

Until 1 March 2000, sleepy Aberdeen, on the New England Highway 266 km north-northwest of Sydney, population 1750, was best known as the birthplace of the blue heeler cattle dog, the canine icon that is as much a part of Australian folklore as the emu, koala and kangaroo.

But not any more. These days Aberdeen is known as the home of Katherine Knight, arguably the most depraved female killer in Australia's history. Visitors to Aberdeen are now far more interested in seeing the single-storey three-bedroom bungalow at 84 Andrew Street, where a murder and other unspeakable acts took place, and pondering what would cause the middle-aged housewife, mother and grandmother to perpetrate such evil.

Katherine Knight was born half an hour after her twin sister, Joy, at Tenterfield Hospital in northwestern New South Wales on 24 October 1955. Her mother, Barbara, already had four boys — Patrick, Martin, Neville and Barry — by a previous marriage, and another son, Charlie, with Katherine's father, Ken. One more son, Shane, would follow in 1961.

When Barbara's previous marriage had broken down, the two older boys, Patrick and Martin, stayed with their father, Jack Roughan, and the two younger lads, Neville and Barry, went to live with an aunt in Sydney. When Jack Roughan died, in 1959, Patrick and Martin returned to live with their mother.

Ken Knight was an abattoir slaughterman who travelled with his family throughout Queensland and New South Wales doing his back-breaking trade in 12-hour shifts. They lived at Wallangarra, Gunnedah, Tenterfield and Moree — wherever the work was to be found. Ken and Barbara and their six children eventually settled in Aberdeen in 1969; there was steady work at the local abattoir.

By all accounts young Katherine was a loving little girl who was kind to animals. Her only brush with the law occurred when she was a 13-year-old: she appeared before the Children's Court on a minor charge and received a good behaviour bond.

Given her home environment, it's hardly surprising that all Katherine Knight wanted to do when she grew up was work in the abattoirs. Every town she had ever lived in had had a meatworks.

At 16 she joined her father, twin sister, Joy, and brother Charlie at the Aberdeen abattoir; her job was boning out carcasses. In the predominantly male domain, Katherine became as tough as the best of them, and gave as much as she got in the boning-floor jargon — which would make a wharfie blush. She was renowned for not taking a backward step, and with her knife in her hand she'd propose armed combat to anyone who offended her. No one ever took her on. Katherine's proudest possession was her set of razor-sharp boning knives, which she kept above her bed.

Given her future violence, it would be fair to say that this period in her life probably played a major role in the moulding of Katherine Knight.

In 1973 Katherine fell in love with 22-year-old truck driver David Kellett. As soon as she turned 18 she moved in with him, and in 1974 they were married. A local rumour was that Katherine attempted to strangle her husband on their wedding night when he wouldn't make love to her often enough.

In May 1976, shortly after their first child was born, Kellett, unable to cope with his wife's possessiveness and violent, moody behaviour, took off with another woman.

Deeply depressed and vengeful, and with no one else to take her grievances out on, Katherine Kellett chose the closest thing to her. One day shortly after David had left, she walked down to the local train line and left her 2-month-old daughter in the middle of the tracks, to be run over by the next train that came along. Fortunately the infant was rescued — a man foraging nearby heard her crying.

Later that same day, Katherine took an axe from a nearby backyard and, swinging it wildly about her head, threatened to kill several people, including an old man. She was apprehended by police and taken to St Elmo's Hospital in Tamworth, where she was diagnosed with postnatal depression and released.

A few days later Katherine slashed the face of a woman she knew with a butcher's knife while demanding that the woman drive her to David Kellett. Bleeding profusely, the woman only escaped when she pulled into a petrol station. When police responded to a frantic call from the petrol station owner, they found Katherine holding a little boy by the front of his shirt and waving a knife in the air.

The officers managed to drag the terrified child away by attacking Katherine with a couple of brooms that were nearby. They grabbed her when she dropped the knife and let the boy go. On the recommendation of a local doctor, she was admitted to Morisset Psychiatric Hospital for treatment; her baby daughter was placed in the care of her grandparents, Barbara and Ken Knight.

Police notified David Kellett, who was working in Queensland, that his wife had been committed to psychiatric care and was locked in a ward and under heavy sedation. With his mother, Jean, Kellett drove down — it was hundreds of kilometres — to be with his troubled wife. She sparked up the minute she saw him.

On 9 August 1976, Katherine was released into the care of her mother-in-law, on the condition that Jean made sure she took her medication. They collected the baby along the way. Within a couple of weeks Katherine and David were back living together in a rented bungalow in Woodridge in Queensland. David drove trucks and Katherine took a job boning at the Dinmore meatworks in Ipswich.

The relationship was stormier than ever now, with Katherine regularly flying into violent rages over nothing in particular and assaulting her husband with her fists, kitchen appliances and anything else she could lay her hands on. Yet, despite all this, on 6 March 1980 they had another daughter.

And then, one day in 1984, as if in answer to David Kellett's prayers, she was gone. He came home one night from work and the house was bare. Katherine had packed up her two daughters and everything that wasn't nailed down and moved back to live with her parents on their farm outside Aberdeen.

Back working at the Aberdeen abattoir and having resumed her maiden name, Katherine Knight didn't last long down on the farm with the folks; she moved with the two children to a rented property in nearby Muswellbrook. A year later her back gave out, due to constantly bending over the carcasses at the abattoir, and she had to give up working altogether.

The government found her a Housing Commission house in Aberdeen, which suited her down to the ground: it was close to the girls' school, so the girls could walk instead of having to be driven every day. With a pension as income, the only thing the tall, thin, attractive 30-year-old Knight now needed was a man.

After several brief and unsuccessful relationships, Knight clicked with Dave Saunders in a local hotel in 1986. Saunders, a 38-year-old miner from nearby Scone, was considered a good bloke whose only problem was that he liked a drink and spent most of his time at the hotel getting a skinful.

For all her shortcomings — such as attacking people with knives, fists and kitchen appliances — Knight had a cheery and charming exterior, and the ruggedly handsome Saunders was smitten. The fact that she had a voracious sexual appetite was the icing on the cake.

Things went along lovingly for a few months. Dave Saunders kept his apartment at Scone but moved in with Knight and her two daughters. However, it didn't take long for the green-eyed monster to come out in Knight, and soon she was constantly (incorrectly) accusing her de facto of having affairs with other women. From then on they were always at each other's throats. Katherine would throw Saunders out of her house, but no sooner would he arrive back at his place in Scone than she would be knocking on the door begging his forgiveness and asking him to come back — which he always did.

It wasn't long before the fights got violent, with Knight, who was taller than her man, getting stuck into him with her fists and boots. In May 1987 she let him know what would happen to him if he ever played up with another woman: she slit his 2-month-old pup's throat from ear to ear with a boning knife before taking to Saunders with a frying pan and bashing him into unconsciousness.

But despite Katherine's continuing violent and bizarre behaviour, which included a suicide attempt, Saunders' love proved unfailing, and in June 1988 Katherine gave birth to her third daughter.

With the arrival of the new baby, a calm settled over the little family. Saunders put a deposit on a tiny house in Aberdeen and Knight paid it — and Saunders — off in full when the compensation for her back came through in 1989.

The tiny two-bedroom weatherboard house in MacQueen Street, Aberdeen, was the first real possession that the feral Katherine Knight had ever had in her life, so it's hardly surprising that she decorated it exactly the way she wanted to. With her passion: dead animals.

The walls were covered in cow hides, water buffalo and steer horns, old-fashioned fur wraps, cow and sheep skulls and deer antlers. Two stuffed animals — a peacock and a baby deer — had pride of place. Among the other bric-a-brac adorning the walls and hanging from the rafters were a huge wooden fork and spoon, rusted animal traps, leather coats and motorcycle jackets, a rusted rake and pitchfork, a riding boot and crop, and a saddle. Every available space was filled with old newspapers, clothes and books. The extensive video collection dealt predominantly with horror and death.

It was a museum of Katherine Knight's fantasies. There's no place like home.

But as blissful as it was in paradise — with the new baby and the new house filled with Katherine's treasures — it didn't last. In the next bout of exchanges, Knight battered Saunders over the head with an iron and allegedly stabbed him with a pair of scissors. And when he returned to the love nest after another horrific fight and a week in Scone, he was invited in only to be informed that she had cut all his clothes to shreds and taken them to the tip.

This time Dave Saunders decided that he'd had enough. He took his long service leave from the mines and gave all his old drinking haunts a miss. Despite Knight's frantic efforts to find him, she had no luck. His mates knew where he was but they certainly weren't going to deliver him back to the dreaded missus. Running into brick walls everywhere, she eventually gave up.

Months later Saunders returned home to MacQueen Street to see his daughter, only to find that in his absence Kath had gone to the local police and told them that she was terrified he would return and bash her. She'd taken out an Apprehended Violence Order against him to keep him away from her and the kids.

It hadn't taken Katherine Knight long to find another lover, and a few months into this new relationship she was pregnant. The father was local knockabout John Chillingworth, 43, who worked at the Aberdeen meatworks, and the baby, this time a boy, was born in 1991.

Knight's erratic on-again-off-again style of romance saw to it that the relationship only lasted three years (the locals were amazed that it lasted as long as that), and it ended acrimoniously when Kath Knight dumped Chillingworth for John Price, an Aberdeen man she had been having an affair with behind Chillingworth's back for some time.

Although distraught at the time, it turned out that the spurned John Chillingworth was the luckiest bloke on the planet. He would later overcome his broken heart, get off the booze and do something constructive with his life. But by taking up with the wicked witch of Aberdeen, John Price had signed his own death warrant.

By all accounts John 'Pricey' Price was a terrific bloke; he'd give you his left arm if you needed it and was liked by everyone who knew him. He'd been married and had three kids when the marriage broke down in 1988. His wife took their youngest, a 2-year-old girl, when she left and he had their teenage boy and their other girl to look after. He owned a three-bedroom brick bungalow in Andrew Street, Aberdeen, and brought home a good salary from his job in the local mines. The family wanted for nothing.

Pricey met Katherine Knight at a local hotel in 1993. They were the same age, 38, and it wasn't long before they were an 'item' around town. He went into the relationship with his eyes wide open. He had heard all the rumours about the way she treated her men but chose to ignore them.

The relationship started out the same as all of Knight's previous liaisons. She was the devoted, loving spouse who cooked and sewed and picked her man up and drove him home from the hotel when he couldn't walk. Plus she was a passionate lover. His kids got along famously with hers and life was a bunch of roses. But again, it didn't take long for the cracks to start appearing. There were the usual accusations of infidelity, fights, separations and getting back together.

In late 1995 Knight moved into the Price family house in Andrew Street — she kept the other house, though. Price's house must have seemed like living in Buckingham Palace after her cramped little cottage with the dead animals on the walls. The drinking escalated, and so did the fighting. They could be seen yelling at each other in the street outside the front of his house and out the front of her house and at any of the local hotels where they drank. It would be all fun and games one minute and a slanging match the next.

In 1998 Knight showed Pricey's bosses at the mines a videotape she had secretly recorded at home of some items that Pricey had allegedly stolen from work. Knight maintained that she recorded the tape as revenge after a fight about his ongoing refusal to marry her during which they had come to blows and he had belted her. She had at first planned to show the tape to Pricey, to use as blackmail against him. But after another horrendous fight, she decided to go one step further and show it to his employers.

Although all the items on the tape were past their 'use by' date or considered rubbish — they had been scavenged from the company tip — the video was enough to get Pricey the sack from the job that he had had for 17 years.

Pricey booted her out of his home the same day, and she went back to her tiny chamber of horrors in MacQueen Street. The story of her vicious behaviour spread through the tiny township like a bushfire. Given her track record, it didn't surprise a soul.

Price took Knight back a few months later — but he didn't move her back into his house. And he lost a lot of friends; many now wouldn't have anything to do with him when she was in his company.

Their fights resumed, with increased venom. They would get drunk and argue over her getting him sacked from the mine, and it would be on for one and all. It was plain to everyone that while they couldn't live with each other, they couldn't live without each other either. Something had to give; it was just a matter of time.

It wasn't long before Kath had free rein in Pricey's house again. But it didn't help matters in the least. The arguments and violence escalated, and after a series of assaults which included Knight stabbing him in the chest with a knife during an argument in the kitchen, on Tuesday, 29 February 2000, John Price went to the Scone Magistrate's Court and took out an Apprehended Violence Order against her to keep her away from his house — and, he hoped, out of his life once and for all.

But AVO or not, there was no stopping Katherine Knight. On the night he took out the AVO, John Price was in bed at 11 pm, after visiting his neighbours, when a vehicle pulled into his driveway. Knight entered the house, watched TV for a few minutes, had a shower and then joined Pricey in bed. They had sex.

This is the account of what uniformed officers found at the house the following morning:

About 6 am on Wednesday March 1st, a neighbour noticed that the victim's [John Price's] work utility truck was still at his home. This appeared unusual, as the victim normally had left for work each day prior to this time.

This neighbour became concerned, as did the employer of the victim, who was by this time making inquiries as to why the victim had not attended work. Attempts were made by the neighbour and another friend to wake the victim by knocking on his bedroom window. The neighbour and friend then went to the front door, where they saw a small amount of blood on the wooden exterior.

Police were contacted and attended about 8 am. The police at the scene forced entry to the house through the rear door. Upon entry the police located the victim's exterior layers of skin hanging from a hook in a doorway arch into the loungeroom. They then located the victim's decapitated remains on the loungeroom floor near a small foyer leading to the front door.

A further search of the house by police resulted in them locating Katherine Knight, who was snoring loudly in a comatose condition on a double bed at the end of the house. She was removed from the house immediately by police and later conveyed to hospital by ambulance.

The following account is the complete report by crime scene investigator Detective Senior Constable

(DSC) Peter Anthony Muscio, who was the first officer into the premises after the initial discovery of John Price's body. In cases such as this, it is DSC Muscio's job to piece together the macabre facts from the evidence at the murder scene, before anyone else touches a thing.

> About 10 am, Wednesday the 1st of March, 2000, in company with Detective Sergeant Neil Raymond, I attended the premises at 84 Andrew Street, Aberdeen, in relation to an alleged homicide. There I spoke to a number of police, including duty officer Graham Furlonger, Detective Sergeant Bob Wells and Senior Constable Michael Prentice. The premises is a single-storey three-bedroom dwelling which faces generally south onto Andrew Street.
>
> The premises was built towards the eastern side of the block, leaving a grassed area on the western side where three vehicles were parked. These vehicles consisted of a white Toyota 4WD, a white Ford sedan and a white Toyota Landcruiser utility. There were two galvanised steel garden sheds in the rear yard, one at each rear corner. There was also a brick barbeque against the eastern boundary.
>
> The dwelling had a full-length verandah across the southern side and a smaller verandah central to the rear of the premises. My attention was drawn to a piece of cooked meat on the rear lawn in front of the white Ford sedan. I made an examination of this piece of meat and collected it for further testing. During my examination I took a series of photographs of the premises and the piece of cooked meat on the lawn.

I entered the premises to conduct a cursory examination with Detective Sergeant Raymond. I walked in through the rear door and into the kitchen. Once inside the kitchen I saw a large section of what appeared to be human skin hanging from the top architrave of the doorway leading into the loungeroom. This piece of skin extended from the top of the doorway right to the floor and appeared to be an entire human skin.

Looking through this doorway into the loungeroom I could see a headless and skinless human body. I walked east along the hallway and looked into the entry foyer and saw an extreme amount of blood pooled on the floor. There was also a large amount of blood smearing over the eastern wall of the entry.

I walked further east along the hallway and noticed some blood staining leading from the main bedroom. In this bedroom I noticed more blood staining; however, only moderate amounts. I then left the scene and had a discussion with Sergeant Raymond and other investigating police outside the scene. I then re-entered the premises and made a more detailed examination.

The rear door of the premises opens into the laundry, off the western side of this is the kitchen/dining room. The laundry contained a stainless steel tub in the northeast corner and a washing machine further south along the eastern wall. There was a built-in cupboard in two separate wooden louvred doors in the southern wall of the laundry.

On the western wall of the laundry was a cavity sliding door that gave access to the dining room and kitchen. The room was divided into two sections, with the kitchen being the eastern end and the dining room being the western end.

The dining room contained a wood and steel dining room table which had three matching seats placed around it. There were items of clothing draped over the backs of each of the three chairs. On the dining room table was a tool bag, some clothing, a small blue folder, an electronic toy gorilla and some prescription medicine boxes.

I noticed blood staining to the shoulder area of a blue shirt which was draped over the chair on the western side of the table. The medication on the table consisted of three boxes of Felodur ER 5 mg, of which two were empty. This medication normally contains two strips, each containing 15 tablets; however, there was only one full strip containing 15 tablets. There was also one empty box of Prinivil (20 tablets). An empty box of Dapa-Tabs was also on the table. This medication box, when full, contains 90 tablets, each 2.5 mg. The fourth chair of the set was against the northern wall under the bench portion of the breakfast bar. I took a series of photographs of the dining room.

The kitchen was in the east portion of the room. It consisted of a kitchen bench with overhead cupboards along the eastern wall. About central to this bench was an electric cooktop which had a baking dish and an aluminium boiler on it. Along the southern wall was a wall oven and further east was a two-door built-in pantry and a free-standing fridge. Along the northern wall was another bench which incorporated the sink and further west was a breakfast bar that protruded from the northern wall south into the kitchen and divided the kitchen and dining room.

As mentioned earlier, I saw what appeared to be a complete human skin or pelt hanging from the top architrave of the door separating the dining room and the loungeroom. On closer examination I could distinguish black curly hair at the top, a nose and part of the mouth and ears. About halfway down the pelt I could see a clump of short black curly hair consistent with pubic hair. I could not recognise any other particular features as it continued to the floor. The edges of the pelt were incised, indicating to me that it had been removed with a sharp instrument. There were also a number of distinct stab wounds to the pelt, about a metre down from the top. The pelt was attached to the architrave by a stainless steel meat hook. The hook was pierced through the top of the head area of the pelt and then hooked over the architrave on the loungeroom side of the door. The skin appeared to vary in thickness from approximately 1 to 4 centimetres.

I noticed a blood trail leading from the loungeroom into the kitchen towards the kitchen cooktop, in the vicinity of the aluminium boiler. The boiler was on the right-side rear element, which was at the time turned off. When I lifted the lid to the boiler I noticed it was warm to touch.

The pot was full of liquid, and on the surface I could identify a skinned human head and a number of cooked vegetables. On the northern side of the aluminium boiler I saw a baking dish which was sitting across the right front side element. Inside the baking dish I saw an amount of liquid and the remains of baked vegetables. Just to the left or northern side of the cooktop I saw two prepared meals. Each of the meals consisted of two pieces of cooked meat, baked potato, baked pumpkin, zucchini, cabbage, yellow squash and gravy. Underneath each of the meals was a torn section of kitchen paper with a name written on it. The word '——' was written in blue ink pen on one of the pieces while the word '——' was on the other. The pieces of meat that appeared on the plates were similar to the piece I collected from the rear lawn.

On the section of the kitchen bench across the northern wall were a number of items of interest. On the western end of the bench I saw a green electric jug with blood staining about the handle. In the sink I saw an orange-coloured vegetable peeler and the vegetable peelings from potato, pumpkin, zucchini and onion. On the eastern side of the sink I saw a cream-coloured microwave dish containing cooked cabbage leaves and a clearish liquid. In front of the microwave dish I saw a brown-coloured coffee cup which was sitting on a wooden cutting-up board. Inside the coffee cup was a teaspoon and a small quantity of thick brown liquid similar to gravy. There was also the residue of the gravy-type substance on the cutting-up board. Just to the right of the cutting-up board was a yellow-handled 'Swibo' knife and two forks. The handle of the knife was bloodstained.

On the eastern side of the breakfast bar I saw a small black-handled knife which was bloodstained and four empty medication blister packs. One blister pack was labelled 'Luvox' and had 15 tablets missing, two blister packets labelled 'Aropax' had ten tablets missing from each packet and the blister packet labelled 'Promethazine' had 20 tablets missing. I saw a bloodstained grey coffee cup which contained a white fatty substance. There was also an empty Tooheys brand beer stubby, a packet of Winfield Red cigarettes and a black wallet belonging to the deceased on the bench. On the western side of the breakfast bar I saw a Norton brand 'bench stone' sharpening stone.

On the southern side of the cooktop on the bench, against the western wall of the kitchen, was a microwave oven. In front of the microwave were the remains of a roll of paper towel and a blue plastic lid. This lid fitted on the microwave dish that was on the kitchen sink. I also noted that the microwave door was open and the courtesy light was on. On the cork-tiled floor of the kitchen at the southwest corner of the kitchen bench I saw a bloodstained bare footprint. This footprint was from a right foot of a person, and at the time [the footprint was made] the person was standing adjacent to the kitchen bench with the right foot facing north.

I noticed blood staining to the fridge on both the handle of the door to the fridge section and the eastern side of the unit. The staining to the door handle contained some ridge structure and was in a position consistent with opening the door with bloodied hands. There were also smears on the eastern face of the fridge, and lower down, [there was] staining from droplets of blood that had come in contact with this surface.

As mentioned earlier, the loungeroom was off the southern side of the kitchen/dining room, the two rooms being separated by a cavity sliding door. On the eastern side of the loungeroom was an opening 1.6 metres wide, which gave access to the front entry of the premises. The loungeroom contained a single-seat lounge chair in the southeast corner, and further west, against that wall, a three-seater lounge suite, and another single lounge seat in the southwest corner. From this corner, north, against the western wall was a slow combustion heater and another single lounge chair. Along the northern wall from the northwestern corner was a large wooden display cabinet, a smaller display cabinet, the doorway to the kitchen/dining room and single lounge chair in the northeastern corner.

The skinless and headless body of a person now known to me as John Charles Price was in a supine position with his legs protruding into the entry foyer from the knees down. There was a substantial amount of blood smeared over the carpet around the body. As mentioned earlier, there was also an extreme amount of blood pooling on the floor of the entry foyer. In this blood pool and staining were marks where the body of the deceased had been dragged about 1 metre, from about the middle of the entry foyer onto the carpet in the loungeroom. The deceased was lying on his back with his legs crossed at the feet, the left ankle on top of the right. His left arm was extended and out from the body at an angle of about 45 degrees. Under the left wrist of this arm was an empty plastic 1.25 litre Shelleys Club Lemon Squash bottle. The right arm was also extended and lying alongside the body. On the floor, adjacent to the right arm of the deceased, was a bloodstained 31 centimetre yellow plastic-handled knife. The blade of this knife was 17.5 centimetres long. The body was virtually devoid of skin and flesh, exposing the muscles and some organs. There were a number of wounds present on the body, one of the most obvious being a stab wound to the left side of the chest which extended into the chest cavity.

As stated, the body had been skinned in a manner that led me to believe that the person responsible would have had skill in this area. From the blood staining on the carpet I was able to determine that the deceased had been skinned prior to being decapitated. There was a definite outline of the head in the blood staining on the carpet. Examination of the neck region of the deceased indicated that the head had been removed very carefully and cleanly with a sharp instrument.

On the seat of the single lounge chair in the northeast corner of the room (adjacent to the shoulders of the deceased) was a black-handled honing steel (sharpening stone) and an opened packet of Winfield Blue cigarettes. I also noticed bloodied handprints on the back and arms of this chair. On the northern wall on the western side of the door to the kitchen was a small display cabinet. Lying on this cabinet was a broken picture frame containing a picture of the deceased. Lying on top of the picture frame was a bloodstained watch.

It was evident to DSC Muscio that Katherine Knight had murdered John Price, skinned and decapitated him, cooked his head and then served it and portions of his buttocks (the pieces of meat in the backyard also proved to be from the victim's buttocks) on plates for herself and his two children for dinner.

Detective Muscio also said:

I remember walking down the hallway and at about shoulder height there were all these blood splatter

marks on the walls. To me, it's indicative of each attack
... He's absolutely fighting for his life. The bloke's just
had a bonk [sexual intercourse] in the bed when he
wakes up, then stab, stab, stab. He's getting up, there is
arterial spurting on the robe and the bed, and on the
doorway there's a bloodied handprint or swipe on the
western side of the door near the dressing table, and
blood around the light switch. It looks like he's tried
to turn the light switch on. And then all down the
hallway they [bloody handprints] are everywhere. And
he's almost made it. He's opened the front door, but
the screen door is shut. There is blood staining,
trajectory again, flicking out across the front door.
He's almost made it ... but he wouldn't have
survived. He would have been absolutely horrified,
terrified — probably terrified more than horrified —
trying to get out and all the time being stabbed.

An autopsy revealed that the victim was dead
when he was skinned. A razor-sharp knife had been
inserted just under his collarbone and sliced
horizontally across the top of the body, from shoulder
to shoulder, right under the clavicles. It was a
straight, clean cut, anatomically precise. Then the
knife was turned and cut down the chest and over
the stomach to the pubic hair line, and made into a
T with another straight line.

Tracing the knife tip around his pubic area and
careful not to cut his penis or genitals, the killer cut
down the front of John Price's thighs, over the knees
and to his feet. The killer then moved up the body, held
his arms up and cut down the back of each one and
across the top of the victim's head. The killer then

peeled the victim's skin off, including his head, his hair, his face and all the way down the length of the body to the feet, exposing the victim's intestines.

The entire skin was in one piece, including hair, face, ears, nose, mouth and genitals — and stab holes — and dripping in blood. Hanging from the S-hook in the doorway, the feet were dragging on the ground.

The killer then removed the victim's head cleanly at the C3–C4 junction, right at the top of the shoulders, using a very sharp knife. The cut was precise. The killer would have been covered in warm, sticky blood. According to forensic pathologist Dr Timothy Lyons, who performed the autopsy, the whole exercise would have taken about 40 minutes.

Despite intensive questioning, Katherine Knight denied having any recollection of what happened that night after she arrived at the house and had sex with her lover. Having recovered from her alleged suicide attempt, a week later on 6 March 2000, Katherine Knight was charged with John Price's murder at a special bedside sitting in the Maitland District Hospital's psychiatric wing.

In a bizarre twist, it was discovered that after she had murdered her lover, Katherine had gone to an automatic teller machine in Aberdeen and withdrawn $1000 from John Price's bank account.

At her trial in October 2001, Katherine Knight pleaded guilty, which meant that John Price's distraught family did not suffer the ordeal of having to hear all the evidence. According to court-appointed psychiatrists, she was perfectly sane when she committed the crimes.

On 8 November 2001, Justice Barry O'Keefe sentenced Katherine Mary Knight to life imprisonment without the possibility of parole. The judge said that her papers were to be marked 'never to be released'. She has since appealed the severity of the sentence.

It remains unclear whether or not Katherine Knight ate parts of her lover after she cooked his head and slices from his buttocks. It was hard to say if all the pieces of John Price were accounted for. To this day she maintains that all she recalls of that night is that they had good sex and both climaxed. Then she remembers that Pricey got out of bed to go for a pee and she watched him come back into the bedroom. After that she presumes that she fell asleep and that was that.

The general consensus of opinion (and about this case everyone seems to have one) is that she did eat part of John Price and then found what she did so abhorrent that her mind blocked it out — and she now can't, or won't, remember.

In Mulawa Women's Correctional Centre, Katherine Knight works as a cleaner in the governor's office. Although she is a good cook, it is highly unlikely she will ever get a job in the kitchen.

Chapter 12

GOULBURN SUPER MAX

Australia's Toughest Jail

In the tradition of our harsh convict heritage, it seems appropriate that our nation's toughest jail is at Goulburn, arguably one of the bleakest cities in Australia.

Established in 1820 and named after Henry Goulburn, the then Secretary of the State for War and the Colonies, the town is spread over rolling plains just off the Hume Highway, about two hours' drive south of Sydney.

Goulburn was a popular resting place on the drive to and from Canberra until the expressway was built around it. Nowadays most drivers just keep going.

With its population of 24,000, Goulburn claims to be 'Australia's First Inland City' — though Wagga and Bathurst dispute this. The signs could easily claim 'Australia's Coldest City'. In the winter of 2003, amid sleet and light snow, the temperature bottomed out at −7°C.

Once boasting production of some of the finest wool and lamb chump chops in the world, droughts — especially the worst in Australia's recent history, through the late 1990s and early 2000s — have seen to it that Goulburn now depends almost entirely on justice and retribution as its main sources of income.

Founded in 1984, the New South Wales Police Academy, situated just out of town, involves almost 1000 resident police recruits and staff, who give Goulburn much of its cash flow. As do the 350 local residents who work at the jail, which has long been a part of the Goulburn landscape.

A convict lock-up was built at Goulburn in 1830, and in 1883 the James Barnett-designed Goulburn jail was completed, with maximum security accommodation for around 400 inmates.

Mr Barnett was so proud of his prison that tourists were allowed a look through it — for a modest fee — before the gates were officially opened. The highlight of the tour was the gallows, and they were put to plenty of use in the years to come. With the exception of the addition of a new wing called the Multi Purpose Unit, which was completed in 1990, little has changed in the main Goulburn jail since those days.

Given its freezing location, stone and brick structure and lack of proper heating, Goulburn was recognised throughout the penal system as the last place on the planet anyone would want to serve a jail term. And so Goulburn jail became the pits, the final home where New South Wales' worst criminals were sent when nowhere else would have them. The end of the road for serial killers, child murderers, paedophiles and psychopaths, many of whom had committed crimes so appalling that they would never be released from jail, no matter what.

But with this roll-call of outcasts came another problem. Many of them were incompatible with other inmates. When they weren't trying to escape, they were brawling, instigating riots or participating in gang-related drug activities and violence. They were the incorrigibles that no amount of solitary confinement could deter from their reprehensible activities.

It was George Savvas, drug trafficker, armed robber and escape artist — he had escaped from New South Wales and Queensland prisons numerous times over the years — who provided the catalyst for the creation of a prison exclusively for these troublemakers. When Savvas escaped from Goulburn in 1996 and then very nearly escaped twice from Maitland jail — once in the company of notorious serial killer Ivan Milat — even while under close supervision, the Department of Corrective Services and the New South Wales Government were finally convinced that they needed an escape-proof jail exclusively for the worst of the worst.

But it had been tried twice before — at Grafton, and at Katingal, within Long Bay — and had failed miserably both times. In 1978, in the Royal Commission into Prisons in New South Wales, Mr Justice Nagle described some of the brutality of the 'unit for intractables' at Grafton jail, which had operated for 33 years until it had been closed down in 1976:

> Inmates arrived at Grafton customarily attired in overalls and slippers, their arms strapped to their sides by a security belt to which their wrists were handcuffed. In some instances, the beatings began even before the security belt and handcuffs were removed.

The beatings were usually administered by three or four officers wielding rubber batons. The inmate was taken into a yard, ordered to strip, searched, and then the biff began. The word 'biff' by no means describes the brutal beating which ensued.

A former prison officer, Mr J.J. Pettit, described it: 'Sometimes three, four or five of them would assault the inmate with their batons to a condition of semi-consciousness. On occasions the inmate urinates, and his nervous system ceases to function normally.'

If most of the inmates are to be believed, the officers had no compunction about beating them around their backs and heads; nor were they averse to kicking them when they were on the ground. They invariably abused them while they were hitting them, calling them 'bastards', 'cunts' and other abusive names. Sometimes they threatened to kill them.

In the 1978 Royal Commission, Katingal — the window-less, concrete monolith in Long Bay jail that housed up to 40 of the state's most dangerous criminals at a time, under 24-hour constant surveillance — was described as being designed for 'the containment of dangerous violent criminals', and as having been created directly as a result of general dissatisfaction with Grafton:

Katingal very quickly began to suffer from the same problems as Grafton, for the same reasons; the classification of inmates as 'the worst 1 per cent' allowed the abuse of authority that led to unacceptable conditions.

The Hon. Dr Meredith Burgmann, MLC, later described Katingal as 'the high-tech unit at Long Bay jail which is so high tech that it now cannot be converted to any other purpose. Indeed, it is built so strongly and is such a terrible obscenity of concrete and iron bars that it would cost a great deal to even demolish it.'

Katingal was closed in 1978 following the recommendations of the Nagle Report. But not before bank robber and gunman Russell 'Mad Dog' Cox had escaped from the 'inescapable' fortress and spent 11 years on the run. Cox escaped in 1977, and was recaptured after a shootout with police in Melbourne in 1988.

And so, with the failures of the past in mind and brutality no longer a part of Corrective Services culture, a panel of architects was appointed, overseas fact-finding trips were made, and the plans for the new building at Goulburn jail were eventually drawn up. Australia's Alcatraz would be constructed within the walls of the jail, but it would be an entirely separate unit from the existing prison.

The fortress would be known in prison-speak as the HRMU — High Risk Management Unit. But to the public it would be 'Super Max' — the American generic term for a mega-maximum security unit within a maximum security prison. It would not house any minor offenders.

To keep close tabs on Super Max, the facility would come under the immediate jurisdiction of two of the most experienced and respected Corrective Service officers in the country: Regional Commander Brian Kelly and Goulburn jail governor John Dunthorne.

On 1 June 2001, New South Wales Premier Bob Carr opened Super Max for business, and showed his new baby off to the media before the inmates were moved in.

If getting out of Super Max is considered impossible, getting in isn't much easier. Anyone entering the facility — the Premier included — is searched and scanned at each of three points before entry.

Between the razor-wired outer wall that surrounds Super Max and the prison itself is a 10 metre wide moat. But unlike the castles of old, this moat contains no water. It is filled with sharp rocks that make crossing in regulation prison footwear all but impossible.

Super Max consists of three separate fully enclosed units; there are 75 cells all told. To date it has never been close to full — the maximum has been 42 inmates.

All units — and all of the cells — are air-conditioned and centrally heated. Each of four cells in a unit adjoins an unbreakable and bullet-proof polycarbonate glass-enclosed 'day room' which is in full view from a circular ground level command post a few metres away. The command post is enclosed in bullet-proof glass. There are six day rooms, side by side, making a circle. Every inmate must enter the day room to which his cell is attached, and be in full view of officers, before there is direct contact between the inmate and an officer. Prisoners can sit in the day room that their cell is attached to, on their own, and they can use the microwave in there, again on their own.

Inside the command post, prison officers monitor every inch of the unit on video screens. But there are no video cameras in the cells. The floors are highly polished linoleum and the air is at a constant 22°C. It feels more like a motel, quite different from the freezing old convict jail just a few hundred metres away. Standing here, I find it almost impossible to believe that I am at the nucleus of a maximum security prison.

I am only the second journalist ever to be taken into Super Max while it is operational. (After nine months of applications, approval has ultimately been granted by New South Wales Prisons Commissioner Ron Woodham.) I have made it clear that I am not interested in the inmates individually, but in the day-to-day running of the facility. I have been taken to a unit that currently contains only three inmates, of whom I only catch glimpses as they exercise.

My escort is Goulburn jail governor John Dunthorne, a no-nonsense veteran of 27 years in Corrective Services and past governor of some of the toughest facilities in Australia, including the Metropolitan Remand and Reception Centre at Silverwater in New South Wales, and Townsville and Woodford Correctional Centres in Queensland.

'In no other facility in Australia is there a concentration of this profile of inmate,' Dunthorne says. 'These are criminals who simply cannot be managed in a mainstream prison environment. They need a higher level of security than any others.'

'My staff do a magnificent job in managing these difficult inmates,' he continues. 'They also receive an enormous amount of respect throughout the local community for the important job that they do.'

Although I'm surrounded by the worst criminals in the New South Wales prison system, the environment isn't threatening. In Super Max I don't experience the anxiety — or was it fear? — that I have experienced in other maximum security prisons. I feel perfectly safe.

Then I realise why. Unlike Grafton or the main Goulburn jail, where the officers mingle with the inmates, in Super Max, all interaction is controlled. While inspecting other maximum security units I have actually spoken to some of the inmates, and I found that intimidating.

There is none of that here. A minimum of three guards must be in attendance during any direct contact with an inmate. I will not be allowed anywhere near the inmates, nor they near me. I don't mind in the least.

The men and women officers are immaculately groomed, and courteous and informative when asked to explain their particular function in the unit. I know they're not putting it on just because I'm with the governor. I've been in enough jails to know that the officers of the modern Corrective Services are a million miles removed from the blood and guts image of old.

I spent a year in and out of Cessnock jail when I was interviewing serial killer William MacDonald for my book *The Knick-Knack Man: Inside The Mind of Australia's Most Deranged Serial Killer*, and the officers didn't have to bung on any side for me — I was just an author — but they treated me like royalty, and I'll never forget them for it.

The same thing applied in Long Bay and Grafton jails when I did a story for *60 Minutes* about the longest serving inmates in Australia. Nothing I asked for was a problem for the officers before, during and after the shoot.

After we have inspected the command post, Governor Dunthorne suggests I stand in the area between the command post and the day rooms and tell him what I hear. After a minute I have to admit that I can hear nothing at all.

'That's the noise of no noise at all,' he says. 'Now you can say that you've actually stood somewhere and heard nothing at all. No radio or TV. No computers, no cars in the background. No one talking. No phones ringing. None of the normal, everyday noises you would hear if you stood somewhere — anywhere — and closed your eyes and just listened.

'That's the way it is in here. Inside the glassed-in day rooms and cells they have their own noise. In the command post we have our noises. But out there, in between, there's nothing.'

He is right. This is another planet. I remember once when I was at a Stephen King lecture he said that he had just ridden his Harley-Davidson across the Nullarbor Plain, and he had stopped in the middle and just stood there and listened — and heard nothing.

He said it was the eeriest place he had ever been. The only place he had ever been on the planet where he could stand and not hear a God-damned thing. Of course he said it would make a great place for a movie of one of his books.

And I have just experienced that same sound. The noise of no noise at all.

'The rule in here is that we can be civil with the inmates but we don't have friends outside of ourselves,' Dunthorne says. 'We try to make it as livable as possible for the inmates — within the regulations, and depending on what behaviour phase the inmate is on.'

Each cell contains a concrete bed, a foam mattress, pillows and blankets, a toilet and a shower recess. There is a small individual exercise yard at the rear of each cell, with a concrete bench. The outlook is onto a concrete wall.

There are no taps or light switches in the cells. To turn the shower and the lights on and off, the inmate must ask the officer through an intercom on the wall. There are no sharp edges to inflict self-harm and nowhere to hang a noose.

After a two-week assessment, inmates can earn privileges — there are three phases they have to work through. Those who rebel are allowed only the bare essentials that the law requires. Prisoners who reach phase three can watch their own TV (either purchased in jail or rented), read books and listen to the radio.

Phase three inmates are allowed one phone call a week, one one-hour visit a week and can have up to $100 per month put into their bank account by friends and family — with this money they can buy cigarettes, books, sweets, CDs and the like from the supervised prison 'buy up'. If they don't have anyone to give them money, they make do on the normal prison wage of $12.75 a week.

At a phase three inmate's request, he will be allowed to associate with other inmates — though only one at any time, and under strict supervision. A small external exercise yard with a basketball hoop and walking track can be used for up to one hour a day — once again, under strict supervision. And while they are there, prisoners may — if they are lucky — hear a bird, or even the wind in a distant tree.

If an inmate strays one iota outside the rules, he is busted back to phase one and has to earn his privileges all over again.

Life in Super Max begins at 8 am with a staff briefing. Then the inmates' breakfasts of cereal, fruit, and coffee or tea are delivered to their cells on trays. Lunch of sandwiches and fruit are delivered at noon, and dinner (a meal that can be heated up later in the microwave in the day room or a salad and fruit) is delivered at 3.30 pm. Then it's shutdown until the next morning.

All meals are prepared outside Super Max and delivered in plastic containers on trolleys. All meals are X-rayed when they are delivered. No inmate has a designated meal, so officers can be certain that a meal containing contraband cannot find a particular inmate.

Only after he has proved himself to be ready for re-integration will an inmate be moved back into the mainstream prison population. Having seen both — Super Max and maximum security in the main Goulburn jail — if I could learn to handle the solitude, I would rather be in Super Max.

One of the first inmates to be moved into Super Max was Australia's most notorious serial killer, Ivan Milat. Milat is the infamous Backpacker Murderer, who between 1989 and 1992 tortured and murdered seven young backpackers and concealed their bodies in the Belanglo State Forest in the New South Wales southern highlands.

After several escape attempts and numerous ploys — such as swallowing razor blades — to get himself into the prison hospital from where escape was deemed easier, Milat wound up in Super Max, where his activities have been curbed.

The perpetrator of the Central Coast Massacre, 56-year-old Malcolm George Baker, is another resident at Super Max. His case was covered in *Never To Be Released Volume 2*.

In October 1992, Baker went on a one-night rampage with a shotgun at Terrigal, on the New South Wales Central Coast. By the time he walked into the nearby Toukley police station to confess, he had killed six people, including a woman who was eight months pregnant and his own ex-de facto wife.

Baker was sentenced to life without the possibility of parole, and before he arrived at Super Max he had been a handful.

'Malcolm Baker had the ideal criteria for entry to the HRMU,' says Governor Dunthorne. 'He is a potential psychopath, and was a threat to anyone he came in contact with. And that was staff or inmates. Now he is under control and no threat to anyone.'

Other Super Max residents are gangster and multi-murderer Michael Kanaan and some of his gang, who are described in this book. Kanaan was violent and uncontrollable in a normal maximum security prison environment, and a threat to anyone and everyone he came near.

Also under the watchful eye of Dunthorne and Super Max superintendent Mark Wilson and his team is another violent psychopath, Lindsey Robert Rose. Dubbed the St Valentine's Day Killer, Rose — who also featured in *Never To Be Released Volume 2* — was a contract killer who murdered five people. Among his victims were two prostitutes he killed in a brothel on

St Valentine's Day, 1994. Rose then set the brothel on fire and fled.

But the Super Max inmate who has achieved more notoriety in recent times than any other is serial gang-rapist Bilal Skaf. In August 2000, the then 18-year-old Skaf was the leader of a pack of up to 14 Sydney western suburbs teenagers who carried out some of the most violent and abhorrent rapes this country has ever seen.

The modus operandi was this: members of Skaf's gang would persuade teenage girls to go somewhere with them, and then they would take the girls to secluded spots and rape them. Then they would call other gang members — who were waiting nearby — on their mobile phones and invite them to come and join in. One victim had a gun held to her head and was told she would be killed if she didn't cooperate.

After Skaf and his gang had finished with their victims, the girls would be dumped and threatened with death if they went to the police. One girl was hosed down as she lay sobbing hysterically after being raped 25 times by 14 youths over a six-hour period.

Skaf was unrepentant throughout his trial: he offered no defence, showed no contrition or remorse and treated the whole procedure as a joke. He was found guilty of being the ringleader in three cases, which included a series of gang rapes in the one night.

The individual offences for which Skaf was found guilty were rape, assisted rape, assault and detainment — there were 23 offences in total. Added together, his sentences come to 280 years. He was sentenced to 55 years in jail (this is the longest of all his individual sentences), with a minimum non-parole period of 40 years.

(In October 2002, Bilal Skaf's brother Mohammed, who was 16 at the time of the offences, was sentenced to 32 years with a non-parole period of 20 years for his part in the rapes.)

In handing down the sentence, Justice Michael Finnane said: 'The offender's head sentence will conclude on 11 February 2056 and his non-parole period will conclude on 11 February 2040. At this stage he will have been in custody for 40 years. Hopefully he will no longer be a menace to society.'

Even while in custody on remand, Bilal Skaf was a difficult inmate. He was immature, uncontrollable, and the target of every Lebanese Muslim inmate in the system — because he had brought disgrace upon his countrymen. Once he was sentenced, he was sent straight to Super Max.

But even in there Skaf wasn't quiet. It seemed he was seldom out of the newspapers. First, cartoons he drew in prison depicting extreme sexual violence against women, including the pack rape of his former fiancée after his engagement came to an end (while he was in prison), were released to the media.

Then he allegedly sent his ex-fiancée a series of threats; this only ended after the woman complained to the Department of Corrective Services.

Then Skaf's father, Mustapha Skaf, was banned from visiting his son in jail after he (Mr Skaf) allegedly tried to bribe a prison officer to place a phone call to his son. Then Skaf's mother was banned from visiting her son for two years after she allegedly tried to smuggle out correspondence which contained sketches of his cell and the exercise yard. Bilal Skaf was banned from receiving visitors for a month over that incident.

Then Skaf was charged with 'sending an article with the intention of inducing another person to falsely believe that the article would explode or be harmful to themselves or property', after he allegedly sent a white powder laced letter to Correctional Services Commissioner Ron Woodham.

When Skaf was due to appear in Yass Court on the above charge, a caller to Goulburn jail threatened to shoot court staff if Skaf was not released within three days. It was understood that the man claimed to be from W2K — Willing to Kill — the same gang which allegedly plotted the (foiled) escape of political assassin Phuong Ngo, who was convicted of the 1994 murder of politician John Newman in Sydney.

On 18 December 2003, in the Downing Central Local Court, the alleged 'white powder' charge against Skaf — which had been reduced to a charge of threatening prison staff — was dismissed on the grounds that there was no prima facie case to answer due to lack of evidence.

But though Skaf is still a handful, we can all rest easy that he is safely locked away, along with New South Wales' other most violent criminals, in Super Max.

Never To Be Released
Volume 2

PAUL B. KIDD

Murderers, rapists, psychopaths ... In many parts of the world, these sorts of criminals can expect retribution by firing squad, lethal injection, the noose or, more macabrely, the electric chair. In Australia, our courts sentence them to a life of incarceration — 'never to be released'.

This recommendation is usually reserved solely for the worst of the worst: the child killers, those who rape and murder in pairs and packs, the serial killers, the mass murderers. But now that list includes a man who attempted to murder a tourist, another who set a little boy alight, and a heroin dealer.

In this frank and compelling book, Paul B. Kidd, a respected authority on this gruesome rollcall of humanity, looks at recent cases that have resulted in the handing down of a 'never to be released' recommendation or its equivalent, the threads that link Australia's serial killers, and the arguments for and against capital punishment.

All the horrific crimes in this book actually happened. Fortunately, all their perpetrators are where they belong — behind bars — 'never to be released'.

ISBN 0 7322 5981 9

The Knick-Knack Man

PAUL B. KIDD

Inside the mind of Australia's most deranged serial killer what do we find?

'Signature' serial killers are the rarest of all multiple murderers. On each victim they leave their unmistakable signature, or 'calling card', so that their pursuers know that the killing is the handiwork of the same offender.

So rare are captured signature serial killers that access to them by anyone other than the authorities is seldom granted. To find a signature serial killer who is both accessible and willing to talk about his crimes is all but impossible.

For these reasons, no signature serial killer has ever told his story in intricate detail to an author.

To write this book, Paul B. Kidd, an acknolwedged authority on Australia's serial killers, spent many hours in prison with Australia's most infamous signature serial killer and probed deep into his mind to reveal for the first time why he committed such unimaginable crimes.

Victim by victim, the killer tells in his own words every bone-chilling detail of the murders and why he performed his unique ritual on their corpses.

ISBN 0 7322 7058 8